The Macat Library
世界思想宝库钥匙丛书

解析大卫·休谟
《人类理解研究》

AN ANALYSIS OF
DAVID HUME'S
AN ENQUIRY CONCERNING HUMAN UNDERSTANDING

Michael O' Sullivan ◎ 著
王弋璇 ◎ 译

上海外语教育出版社
SHANGHAI FOREIGN LANGUAGE EDUCATION PRESS

目 录

引 言 1
 大卫·休谟其人 2
 《人类理解研究》的主要内容 3
 《人类理解研究》的学术价值 5

第一部分：学术渊源 7
 1. 作者生平与历史背景 8
 2. 学术背景 12
 3. 主导命题 15
 4. 作者贡献 18

第二部分：学术思想 23
 5. 思想主脉 24
 6. 思想支脉 28
 7. 历史成就 32
 8. 著作地位 36

第三部分：学术影响 39
 9. 最初反响 40
 10. 后续争议 44
 11. 当代印迹 48
 12. 未来展望 52

术语表 55
人名表 57

CONTENTS

WAYS IN TO THE TEXT	63
Who Was David Hume?	64
What Does *An Enquiry Concerning Human Understanding* Say?	65
Why Does *An Enquiry Concerning Human Understanding* Matter?	67
SECTION 1: INFLUENCES	71
Module 1: The Author and the Historical Context	72
Module 2: Academic Context	77
Module 3: The Problem	81
Module 4: The Author's Contribution	85
SECTION 2: IDEAS	89
Module 5: Main Ideas	90
Module 6: Secondary Ideas	95
Module 7: Achievement	100
Module 8: Place in the Author's Work	105
SECTION 3: IMPACT	109
Module 9: The First Responses	110
Module 10: The Evolving Debate	115
Module 11: Impact and Influence Today	120
Module 12: Where Next?	125
Glossary of Terms	129
People Mentioned in the Text	131
Works Cited	134

引 言

要 点

- 大卫·休谟（1711-1776）是苏格兰哲学家。
- 休谟出版于1748年的《人类理解研究》是关于我们对世界信仰起源的描述。
- 该书是英国经验主义*哲学传统中最伟大的作品之一。

大卫·休谟其人

大卫·休谟1711年出生在苏格兰爱丁堡市的一个并不算富裕却仍是贵族的家庭。年轻的学者休谟12岁就进入爱丁堡大学读书。但是他毕业时却没有拿到学位，后来也未能在大学中谋得教职，多少也是因为他的宗教思想。休谟不接受基督教的思想。事实上，他可能根本不相信上帝，而当时的苏格兰的大学受制于苏格兰教会*，持有他那样的宗教观点的人当然不可能被视为模范雇工。

他于是成为了一名外交家和作家。很快，他被很多人视为苏格兰启蒙运动*的领军人物，这段时间也是科学和文学在苏格兰兴盛发展的时期。休谟结识了爱丁堡、伦敦和巴黎许多引领时代的知识分子，并在法国乡村著书立说，从事哲学写作。1738年，他出版了第一部著作《人性论》，介绍了他的人类思想理论。这部书刚出版的时候并不畅销，于是休谟撰写了更简短和大众化的引言介绍他的观点，即《人类理解研究》。1754年他作为热销书《大不列颠史》的作者而闻名于世。

休谟晚年在一本书中质疑了对上帝的信仰。1776年，休谟去世后，该书以《自然宗教对话录》之名在爱丁堡出版。休谟认为书的主题有很强的争议性，因此选择在身后出版。

虽然很多人认为休谟是用英语写作的哲学家中最伟大的一位，而他在有生之年却更多是因为历史学家的身份而被人了解和认识。他是英国经验主义哲学运动中最后一位伟大人物，该运动强调了经验在人类思想和知识体系中的重要作用。

《人类理解研究》的主要内容

休谟通过他的哲学尝试理解科学未能解释之事，也就是人类思想的运作机制。尽管现代科学已经在理解世界方面取得了巨大进步，但意识领域仍然有很多未被发掘之处。休谟着力改变这一现状，以科学原则探索我们对思维行为的思考方式。

休谟认为，我们很多对世界的信念既非来源于经验，也非来源于理性，而是源自思想行为的方式。简言之，我们因人之本性而拥有行为的信念。

休谟以经验主义的原则，即意识中的所有之物不是印象*就是观点*，展开了论证。这里的"印象"大致指的是感知经验，而"观点"则是印象的复制。举例来说，假设你看到了一个红苹果，看到这个苹果时，你获得了对它的印象。但当你回想这个苹果时，即使是转瞬之后，你所记住的是从印象复制而来的观点。

休谟指出，我们是通过相信因果关系而理解经验。但是我们相信这种所谓"因果"的观点本身并不源于任何经验。在休谟看来，它来源于思维的特定习惯。举例来说，我们习惯于期待未来如同过去一样，但是这种习惯并不因经验而成立；我们创造它皆因人性使然。

这就让休谟开始走进认为真知不存在的哲学流派——怀疑论*的领域。休谟认为，如果我们对世界的信念不来自经验，那为何会有这些信念？我们能否获知对世界的认识？在休谟看来，哲学推理可以表明我们不能。但人们需要形成对世界的信念从而生活下去。由于对因果的信念，也就是甲导致乙的逻辑，过于接近人性的内核，而无法被哲学论证摧毁。

休谟受到先前的哲学家，特别是英国经验主义者约翰·洛克*的影响。洛克相信包括思想、感知或情绪在内的感官经验产生观点，我们也在意识中保有这些观点。举个例子，我们只有看到了某种颜色才可能了解它。洛克认为，通过求证观点由何种经验所导致，我们可以理解意识中的一切，包括信念。

之后的哲学家，如伊曼努尔·康德*认为休谟推动经验主义得出符合逻辑的结论：如果经验主义是理解事物的可靠方法、如果每个观点都需要被证实并得到科学论证的话，我们就无法得出对世界的任何真知灼见。这些哲学家认为休谟不经意间证明了由于经验主义的逻辑结论是怀疑论，而因存在可以确知的事物，所以怀疑论是荒谬的，因此经验主义是不可能成立的。例如，我知道我的名字，也知道伦敦是英国的首都。20世纪中期，哲学家伯特兰·罗素指出，休谟的哲学推理指向"死胡同；沿着他的理论方向，不可能走得更远"。

休谟近期的学生却以不同的方式诠释他的思想，他们不以彰显知识可知或不可知这一方式去理解他。他们认为，休谟实际上是在践行着心理学，以此凸显思维如何工作。休谟并不是问信念正确与否，而是去问我们为什么有这些信念，信念从何而来。[1]

《人类理解研究》的学术价值

休谟的论证全程呼应了之后的哲学、心理学及科学的思考,其历史重要性不能被否认。

心理学史认为休谟的论证通过使用科学手段理解人类思维是具有开创意义的尝试。虽然后来的心理学家采用更为复杂的思维模块,但休谟的思维理论仍然是颇有影响力的早期尝试。

在哲学这一学科领域,休谟对认识论*,即对知识的研究这一领域,做出了贡献。他提出了人类如何获取知识这一问题,并表明我们对世界的信念比我们想象中的更不可靠——经验本身并不能解释这些信念。

休谟同样对存在上帝的信仰提出了质疑,认为我们没有充足的理由相信上帝存在,或者神迹*会发生。这些是基本的问题,却仍然存有争议。

如今,我们通常认为科学是理解世界和增进知识的最好方法。休谟会同意这一点,因他是科学世界观的早期倡议者。但是我们认为科学基于证据;休谟挑战了这一假设。在他看来,证据本身并不能解释科学信念,证据和科学主张之间总有一道鸿沟。想理解科学本身问题的哲学家和科学家们都需直面休谟的论争。

更概括地说,休谟的方法为我们质疑自己对世界的信念提供了好的路径。休谟总是叩问我们的信念来自何处及信念为何而生。他探寻我们在经验世界中信念的根源,也教会我们可以适用于任何信念的批评方法。即使我们不同意休谟的理论,我们仍可以用这种理论来检验我们的信念。

休谟的《人类理解研究》一书文笔优美,其散文写作手法值得一读。此书很好地解释了为何很多人将休谟视为最伟大的哲学作家之一。

---

1. 伯特兰·罗素:《西方哲学史》,伦敦:劳特利奇出版社,2004年,第600页。

第一部分：学术渊源

1 作者生平与历史背景

要点

- 《人类理解研究》是研究人类思维工作机制最有影响力的著作之一。
- 休谟来自一个虔诚的基督教家庭,但在青年时期,他在学习哲学,特别是与意识相关的哲学时远离了宗教。
- 他写作的时期正值知识大发展的年代,被称为苏格兰启蒙运动。

为何要读这部著作?

很多人都将大卫·休谟出版于1748年的《人类理解研究》视为英国经验主义哲学传统的最佳典范。经验主义认为所有人类知识都来自经验。经验主义者相信所有存在于意识中的万事万物都来自我们的感受;休谟将思维的要旨,特别是人的信念,一直追溯到感观经验上的根源层面。

休谟的结论同怀疑主义哲学一致:都认为世界上真正的知识是不可能获得的。在他看来,经验不能成为我们对世界的认识背后的原因,相反,在很大程度上,我们的经验源自某些思维习惯。这些思维习惯可以解释我们的信念,但却无法为这些信念提供合理的缘由。休谟认为,我们不得不被动地接受一些信念,是因为没有它们,实际生活将不可行。

这种论争对思想哲学和心理学领域都非常重要。休谟对思维提出了富有自然主义*色彩的描述。在哲学领域,自然主义认为哲学和科学都试图以生活本来的样子理解生活。18世纪中期,休谟从事写作时,像艾萨克·牛顿这样的科学家们已经在理解物质世界方面取得了巨大的进展。休谟希望在思维研究中运用科学的方法,将这种进步拓展到思维领域。

其次,休谟的怀疑论的结论在认识论,也就是知识的哲学研究中十分重要。一些评论者说,休谟的著作表明经验主义得出荒谬的结论(特别是我们不了解因果关系——即一件事情引起另一件事情——的结论)。休谟通过论争所有的知识都依赖于感知经验,无意中(这些评论者这么认为)表明经验主义是错误的。持这种观点最重要的思想家是德国哲学家伊曼努尔·康德,他的著作尝试解释人们推理的方式和他们体验的事物之间的关系。其他人相信休谟的怀疑论在面对人类知识方面揭示了一个基本的问题:对世界真正的认知是不可能的。奥地利哲学家卡尔·波普*就是20世纪这种观点的重要支持者。[1]

> "我发现自己胆大妄为的脾气见长,这让我不喜欢顺从学科中的任何权威,而是指引我建立新方法,从而找到真理。对此经过很多的研究和思考后,最终在我18岁的时候,我面前展开了一幅新的思想蓝图,这让我进入了人生无可估量的境界,并让我带着年轻人天赋的热忱,抛弃一切其他乐趣或营生,全心全意投入其中。"
> ——大卫·休谟:《我生命的某种历史》

作者生平

休谟1711年出生于苏格兰爱丁堡市的一个小贵族家庭。他的父母虽然生活宽裕,但并非大富大贵,因此休谟从来不能依靠家族产业生活;他不得不为了生存而工作。休谟在家庭教师的指导下,年幼时如饥似渴地阅读书籍，他12岁就进入爱丁堡大学读书（当时大部分人14岁入学），虽然他没有拿到学位，但在那里度过了四年时光。[2]

休谟决定以独立学者的身份来谋生。他晚年向爱丁堡大学和格拉斯哥大学提出教职申请，却都被拒绝了。原因可能是他的宗教观，主要是他对上帝的存在提出怀疑，这被认为是异类和危险的。

休谟的第一部主要作品——《人性论》三卷本[3]出版于1739和1740年。这部巨著开始没有很多读者，也没有给学者留下什么印象，休谟因此说过一句著名的话：《人性论》"刚从出版社出生就夭折了。"[4]

为了努力吸引更多的读者关注他的观点，休谟于1748年出版了更简短和容易理解的《人类理解研究》，那时他担任苏格兰军人、政治家詹姆斯·圣·克莱尔*中将的秘书。休谟自己也涉身政治和外交事业，这些工作让他游历了主要的欧洲城市，如维也纳和都灵。他在爱丁堡、伦敦和法国知识界有很多朋友。他曾在法国生活过一段时间。[5]

休谟的六卷本《大不列颠史》出版于1754和1762年之间，成了畅销书，这让他以历史学家而非哲学家的身份而名利双收。休谟于1776年在他的出生地爱丁堡死于腹部癌症，终年65岁。

创作背景

18世纪中期，休谟的家乡苏格兰正处在伟大的科学、哲学和文学知识进步时期，进步之大以至于这个阶段被誉为苏格兰启蒙运动时期。这个时期的重要人物包括经济学家亚当·斯密*（休谟的私交）、科学家詹姆斯·哈顿*以及发明了现代蒸汽机的詹姆斯·瓦特*。休谟活跃在这些圈子里，在这种充满文化和开放氛围的知识分子环境中生活、写作，独立于大学和宗教权威机构。

与大多数当时的苏格兰人一样，休谟的家庭践行着严格刻板的基督教传统。休谟自己说他自小信奉宗教，非常严格地遵循基督教教义。然而，他在大学读了很多哲学和科学书籍后，似乎放弃了宗教。在生命最后的阶段，休谟说，他读过英国哲学家约翰·洛克和塞缪尔·克拉克*6的著作之后就没有再真正地相信过宗教。在他的哲学作品中，休谟似乎在总体上对宗教持怀疑态度，特别是基督教。

由于他的信仰，有些神职人员视休谟为激进分子。关于这一点他们没错。休谟知道他的观点会触怒权威，也不愿冒险让自己的所有作品受到审查，因此他坚持将他最后一部重要的哲学著作放在身后发表，这部讨论宗教和上帝存在与否的著作《自然宗教对话录》[7]出版于1799年，也就是休谟去世后的3年。

---

1. 卡尔·波普：《猜想与反驳》，伦敦：劳特利奇出版社，2002年，第55—61页。
2. 大卫·休谟："我自己的生活"，大卫·菲特·诺顿编，《剑桥休谟指南》，剑桥：剑桥大学出版社，1993年，第351页。
3. 休谟：《人性论》，牛津：牛津大学出版社，1978年。
4. 休谟："我自己的生活"，第352页。
5. 休谟："我自己的生活"，第352—353页。
6. 詹姆斯·鲍斯威尔："我对大卫·休谟先生最后一次访谈的叙述"，查尔斯·维斯和弗雷德里克·波特编，《极端的鲍斯威尔1776—1778》，纽约：麦格劳-希尔，1970年，第11页。
7. 休谟：《自然宗教对话录》，剑桥：剑桥大学出版社，2007年。

2 学术背景

要点 🔑

- 17世纪,艾萨克·牛顿*爵士及其他科学家改变了我们对自然世界的理解。
- 哲学家和科学家们旨在运用新兴的科学手段理解人类思维。
- 休谟受到的影响既来自于以上这些努力,也受到由皮埃尔·贝尔*所复兴的古典怀疑论传统的影响。

著作语境

大卫·休谟的《人类理解研究》充分利用了由前人在17世纪和18世纪所取得的自然科学方面的突破。艾萨克·牛顿的物理系统首次出版于1687年,开创了一套物理世界新概念,它们虽主要属于数学范畴,却基于严格的经验主义实验。新科学用实验和观察的手段来验证结果,开启了方法和理论两方面的革命。新科学也采用一般性原则描述世界,用来解释之前看上去有着显著差异的现象。例如,牛顿的万有引力定律解释了地球表面物体的移动,以及行星的运动。

这个时代的思想家们并没有明确区分哲学和科学。这两者被认为属于同一学科中"自然哲学"和"道德哲学"的两类,前者是对自然世界的研究,包括物理学、天文学、化学和生物学;后者则更加关心人类本身。

在一些像牛顿和罗伯特·波义耳(他在当今被普遍认为是现代化学最早的践行者之一。)*等科学家的主导下,新的科学研究方法在自然哲学领域取得了伟大的成果。但是这种研究方法并没有持续用在道德哲学的研究中。学者们开始梦想将新的科学研究方法延伸至人类社会和经济学以及人类心理学领域。

> "[休谟的著作]目的不仅仅是为了摧毁上帝的形象,还要用人类学取而代之,人类学并不仰望神祇,而是用比较来面对自然世界,用方法来展望科学。人类是自然客体,而非莱布尼茨所言的人是上帝身边的小神;人类是较低等动物之中的伟大动物。"
>
> ——爱德华·克雷格:《上帝的心灵与人类的著作》

学科概览

人类对思想进行研究的渴望由来已久——或许和人类思想的历史一样久远。17世纪,法国哲学家勒内·笛卡尔*理论阐述了"思维的方式"。根据笛卡尔及其追随者的学说,当我们在思考、感觉或者理解某个事物时,思维也同时在大脑中产生观念。内省是对自我思维过程的检查,让我们直接审视这些观念。比如,当我看见一片草地,或者只是想象或想到草地的样子,我就有了绿色这个观念。

一个世纪以后,英国的经验主义用新阐发的科学原则研究人类思维。经验主义者认为心中之物源于经验感知;对他们来说,观念是经由感官进入人类大脑的外部世界的心理表征。休谟在这一传统上最重要的影响来自于英国哲学家约翰·洛克和爱尔兰哲学家乔治·贝克莱*。

洛克将观念追溯到经验感知,他认为世界和我们常识中的概念有很大差异，只有通过自然科学，我们才可以发现世界的真正的本质所在。贝克莱甚至提出一个更为激进的观点，他认为物质世界根本不存在，也就是说，除了观念和产生观念的思维，包括上帝的旨意，其余皆不存在。

学术渊源

休谟很喜欢阅读笛卡尔、洛克和贝克莱以及其对他思维辩论产生影响的哲学家的著述。但他也受到同时代其他思想浪潮的影响，如古希腊思想学派"皮浪怀疑主义"的复兴思潮。法国哲学家皮埃尔·贝尔重新复兴了这一传统。贝尔因他的作品《历史与批判词典》（1697）一书而声名鹊起，休谟经常提及这一作品。

皮浪怀疑主义者认为人类无法获得真理——因为是人总会犯错，我们不应着急做出判断。怀疑主义者认为，与其试图了解这个世界，还不如依照人类的自然本能生活。

贝尔宣扬怀疑主义，但他并不是用知识不可能获得这一普遍原则来推广。相反，贝尔研究了许多不同的信仰体系，包括宗教信仰，他认为，每一种信仰都不确定，都值得怀疑。贝尔因此强调人类理性的局限性，并由此得出结论：因为人类心智总是容易犯错，我们应该容忍不同的观点。他特别指出，我们尤其不可以迫害他人的宗教信仰。

3. 主导命题

要点

- 哲学家和科学家提出思想是怎样运作的问题；尤其是观念从何而来，以及为什么会有观念这样的问题。
- 17 世纪哲学家约翰·洛克认为人类观念是由外在物体引发的；而爱尔兰哲学家乔治·贝克莱则反对这一观点，并且断言外在物体并不存在。
- 休谟尝试提出普遍性原则来解释为什么一些观念会引发其他观念。

核心问题

18 世纪的哲学家探索了思想如何运作的问题。休谟的《人类理解研究》正好顺应了这一传统。

休谟同时代的人认为思想是由观念组成的，也就是，当我们有想法时，精神"客体"就形成了。他们问的一个主要问题是观念是如何及为何会引发其他观念的。他们认为，如果我们了解了这些，我们就可以理解支配思想运作的原理。

这一时期的哲学家以观念来理解所有的精神状态和行动。其核心包括感知和信念。但是同时也涵盖了记忆、情感、愉悦和悲伤以及精神生活所有的其他方面。在每一个实例中，哲学家都会提出疑问：这些观念从哪里来，一种观念是怎样引发外一种观念的？

他们也提出了一个相关问题：我们的观念是否准确地描绘了这个世界？比如说，在感知经验中，我们看到的这个世界是它真正的样子吗？我们对这个世界的信念是真的吗？

因此这个问题部分是研究思想是如何运作的心理学问题,部分是认识论方面的问题,关乎我们能否以及如何获得世界的真知。

> "理解,像人的眼睛,它使我们看到、感知到所有他者,却忽略了本身。需要技巧和努力才可将理解安置在远处,并使之成为自身的目标。"
> ——托马斯·潘恩:《常识》,约翰·洛克:《人类理解论》

参与者

对休谟具有相当重要意义的英国经验主义传统先驱者是约翰·洛克和乔治·贝克莱。这两个思想家都认为,我们的观念源自感知经验。正如一个人若之前从未看到过一种颜色,就不会有对那种颜色的想法、想象或记忆。他们认为我们所有的观念皆类似于此。

这两位思想家继续追问:我们的观念是否的确同外部世界相似。例如,当我看见一片绿地,我的观念之绿同实际存在的绿地是一致的吗?对此,洛克和贝克莱的观点有所不同。

洛克认为观念由外在物体所引发。比如说,你看着绿色的杯子,那么杯子就引发了绿色的观念。

然而,洛克认为观念不完全等同于物体。举例说,你看到的绿色并不实际存在于物质世界中。你对颜色的观念取决于外部世界不同波长反射光的不同质地。因此,尽管我们所持的观念是由外部世界引发,但观念并不总是与外部世界相似。

认为存在观念可以与外部世界相统一的观点被称为"现实主义"*。贝克莱反对现实主义,他提出另外一个观点,这个观点经常被称作"唯心主义"*。贝克莱认为,我们没有理由去假定存在同观念相对应的外部世界。毕竟，我们不可能直接看到这样的世界。我们只能在形成进一步观念的过程中，通过感知经验试着将观念与世界进行比较。

当代论战

休谟同时受到洛克和贝克莱的影响（特别是洛克，休谟经常提及他的名字）。然而，休谟并不认可洛克把所有想法和感知的对象都称为"观念"。休谟认为这样忽略了两者之间重要的区别。

休谟特别区分了感知经验和思想的对象（包括想象和记忆等的对象）之间的不同。他把感知经验的对象称为"印象"，而其他称为"观念"。经验主义的原则认为思想中的所有都来源于感知，休谟用这样的方式表达了这一原则：所有的观念都是印象[1]的复制品。

休谟也想解释为什么头脑会产生特定的观念。假设无论何时我闻到咖啡的香味，我就会想到咖啡的味道。一种想法（咖啡的气味）引发了另外一种想法（咖啡的味道）。休谟想制定一些普遍适用的原则，用以表明为什么想法经常会接踵而至。

休谟有时候会如贝克莱一样，被视为唯心主义者。但是当涉及我们的观念是否和外部的物体相对应这一问题时，休谟既不是唯心主义者，也不是现实主义者——休谟对此毫无兴趣。相反，休谟感兴趣的是想法本身，特别是为什么一个想法会产生另一想法。

---

1. 大卫·休谟：《人类理解研究》，剑桥：剑桥大学出版社，2007年，第14-15页。

4 作者贡献

要点

- 休谟认为我们有关世界的许多信念并非基于理性。
- 休谟既解释了人类理性的运作机制,又展示出其局限性。
- 同时代的其他哲学家通过参照情感而非理性解释了信念(举例说,道德信念)的渊源。

作者目标

大卫·休谟把他的《人类理解研究》描述成为论述"人类本质的科学"[1],是对解释人类思维事实的尝试。休谟认为既然人类具备推理和拥有信念的能力,他希望可以解释为什么我们对世界为产生这样的认知。这个课题兼具积极和消极的意义。一方面,它涉及对人类思维获得一种全新的科学理解;但另一方面,这一课题对人类的多数信念持怀疑态度;因为它辩称我们的许多信念——比如宗教或哲学信念——没有理性的基础。因此,该课题支持了一种怀疑主义,该观点认为世界的真知是不可能的。

自伊曼努尔·康德起,《人类理解研究》作为持续应用于思想研究的经验主义原则,已经打动了很多人。休谟用自己的论证得出结论,哪怕那些结论(类似于怀疑主义)看起来很奇怪或者令人困惑。怀疑主义认为我们普通的日常信念没有现实依据,因而将永远不可能得到对这个世界的真正理解。有些人通过推动经验主义得出逻辑结论,表明如果经验主义是对的,那么怀疑主义也一定是对的,这样使得休谟在无意中削弱了经验主义。

然而，怀疑主义的问题可能成为理解休谟研究课题的一个障碍。休谟的主要目标不是去*改变*我们对世界的信念，而是去*理解*这些信念。他的主要兴趣在于心理学（思维过程的研究），而不是认识论（对知识本身的研究）。如果将休谟主要呈现为试图颠覆那些他认为并非基于推理之上信念因而具有破坏性的哲学家，这就曲解了他的本意。事实上，在休谟著作的结尾部分，他认为，为了俗世生活的正常进行，人们可以在不破坏自己世界观的情况下，接受他的观点。休谟承认，人类自然而然就会形成未经理性证实的观念。比如，当我听到鸟鸣时，我几乎不假思索地就形成了鸟在附近的观点，没有任何哲学观点能阻止我产生这个观点。这只是人性的一部分。休谟并没有指出未经论证而建立的信念有任何问题，也没说过我们应该停止这样做。

> "理性是并且应当是情感的奴隶，并且除了服务和服从情感之外，再不能有其他职能。"
> ——大卫·休谟：《人性论》

研究方法

大卫·休谟对人性，尤其是人类思维进行了科学调查。他想理解人的思维是如何运作的，以及人类为什么会这样思考。他尤其想确认支配人大脑运作的基本原则。他不满足于观察与记录思维现象，而是寻求辨认出大脑思维最基本的特点。

休谟在他的著作的第一章中，就为他的课题辩护，指出这个问题不只是引人入胜，而且是不可回避的。[2] 人们需要对人性有精准且理性的了解，从而达成目标并创造出好的生活。

休谟同时也为自己的兴趣提出一个正当理由。人类出于本性，总是试图理解这个世界，即使这意味着会提出超过人类思维能力所能回答的复杂艰深的理论问题。理解人类思维的极限可以帮我们解决什么问题是我们的脑力可以回答的，什么是不可回答的。这样一来，休谟研究的成功就意味着界定出人类智力的边界。

时代贡献

休谟把他的思维理论视为自己毕生的工作。他在其三卷本的著作《人性论》中首次提出他的理论，但其接受程度令他失望。《人类理解研究》较之《人性论》更简洁易懂，他在其中介绍了他的一些主要观点。

休谟的心理学研究方法可以在弗朗西斯·哈奇森*的著作中找到原型。弗朗西斯·哈奇森是苏格兰哲学家，可以算得上是休谟的导师。哈奇森的研究兴趣特别集中在道德领域（正确与错误背后的原则）和美学（有关自然和美的原则）。哈奇森认为我们有关道德和美的判断不是起源于推理，而是来自于他所谓的"情感"——我们今天将之称为"情绪"。休谟在这一点上和哈奇森的观点一致。但是休谟的研究走得更远。休谟认为无论是在道德和美学领域，还是在我们有关世界的信念方面，包括有关自然的信念在内，推理并没有想象中的那么重要。

哈奇森和休谟通过邮件往来就哲学问题交换意见，休谟非常钦佩哈奇森。但是这段友谊后来破灭了，哈奇森因为休谟的宗教观而反对休谟申请爱丁堡大学的教职。在休谟看来，这非常令人失望。[3]

1. 大卫·休谟:《人类理解研究》,剑桥:剑桥大学出版社,2007 年,第 3 页。
2. 休谟:《人类理解研究》,第 3-23 页。
3. 詹姆斯·摩尔:"哈奇森和休谟",M. A. 斯图尔特和约翰·怀特编,《休谟和休谟的关系》,爱丁堡:爱丁堡大学出版社,1990 年,第 23-57 页。

第二部分：学术思想

5 思想主脉

要点

- 休谟区分了两类问题：观念的连结以及实际的真相。观念的连结与数学密切相关；实际的真相与外部世界相关，需要通过观察和实验才能获得相关知识。
- 休谟认为，我们对因果关系的认识，即一件事情引发另一件事的观点，依赖于思维习惯而非观察。
- 《人类理解研究》用更加简短、更易理解的方式介绍了早期三卷《人类论》中的观点。

核心主题

大卫·休谟在《人类理解研究》中指出，人类从事两类命题，或提问："实际的真相"* 以及"观念的连结。"*1

第二种类型的研究，只有通过推理才能明白观念之间的彼此联系。休谟相信它的唯一有效性依靠数学这门学科。在他看来，除数学之外的一切都需要事实，而事实依靠研究和实验获得。玄学书和神学书并不借用实验结果，仅含有"诡辩术*与幻想"——错误的争辩与想象的真理。他督促我们"将这些著作投入烈火中"。2

他提出的第一类型的研究是关于自然世界一切事物的实际的真相，需要实证研究与实验。遗憾的是，休谟说人类常常抛弃经验知识，而是通过观察对实际真相进行推理。但是观察本身并不能解释为什么我们会持有这些信念。我们经常相信那些仅通过单纯观察不能证实的，特别是同外部世界相关的事情。休谟将此归因于我们相信因果关系。

> "习惯,是人生的伟大向导。只有这条原则可以使经验变得有益,并使我们期待,未来会出现过去曾发生过的一系列类似事情。"
>
> ——大卫·休谟:《人类理解研究》

思想探究

当休谟写下"有关实际的真相的一切推理几乎全部是建立在因果关系之上,"³ 之时他认为,对外部世界的了解存在于因果联系中,即一个事件引起另一事件的发生。例如,当我听到雨滴落在窗户的声音便可以推论出外面正在下雨,我用我所知道的事实知道下雨会有雨滴声。

但是休谟认为,经验永远不足以证明一个事件引发了另一事件。我们所知道的是,遵循一定的规律性和预见性,事情接连发生。仅凭经验,我们不能推断出某一件事是另外一件事发生的原因。假设,在看台球时,我看到一个球的碰撞使另一球移动。休谟指出,严格来说,我所看到的是两个球都移动,而非第一个球导致了第二个球的运动。从休谟的经验主义角度来看,我们并不理解两个桌球之间的因果关系。

那么我们为什么相信因果呢?原因是我们的大脑受他所谓的"习俗和习惯"的支配:休谟谈到,习惯是"人类生活的伟大向导"。⁴ 比如,第一个桌球碰撞第二个桌球,第二个桌球开始移动,当我们注意到这种不同事件之间的"恒常结合",下次看台球时,我们就会下意识地期待发生同样的事情。但是,任何学打桌球的人都知道这种情况并不总是发生。

我们注意到一些模式后（如火是热的，雪是冷的），通常会倾向于期待这些模式在将来保持不变，尽管我们永远无法*证明*这一点。我们期待规律性，并不因为对其拥有经验证据，而是因为期待模式重复发生是我们的天性。休谟得出的结论就是，我们并没有充分理由相信未来会像过去一样。这像我们总是觉得雪是冰冷的，但这并不意味着在我们将来依旧会感觉它是冰冷的。

语言表述

尽管休谟在早期的作品中表达过他的主要观点，他之后提到他"过去始终怀有一个观点，那就是，我期待《人性论》的成功出版更多出自于出版方式而非出版本身"。[5] 休谟将《人性论》写得晦涩难懂，他认为更简短易读的版本将吸引更多的读者。但尽管他是对的，此书还是在他去世后才被大量阅读。

《人类理解研究》语言优美，奠定了休谟即使不是最好的，也是最好的英文哲学散文家之一的地位。纵使现在看来语言有些过时，但用相对简单的英文生动描述，现代读者能够理解。

《人类理解研究》的成功影响了大众对休谟的认识。读者经常认为他对认识论问题兴趣十足（即，探索人类知识的起源、本质以及界限），尤其是关于怀疑论的问题。三卷的《人性论》很明确地指出，这只是休谟关注的一个方面。他的目标，也就是建构人类思维的理论，范围更广，怀疑论仅仅是这个课题中衍生出的问题之一。总体来说，休谟的兴趣更加偏向心理学领域，因为读者要看他们是否能应对综合性更强的《人性论》。

1. 大卫·休谟:《人类理解研究》,剑桥:剑桥大学出版社,2007 年,第 28 页。
2. 休谟:《人类理解研究》,第 144 页。
3. 休谟:《人类理解研究》,第 29 页。
4. 休谟:《人类理解研究》,第 45 页。
5. 大卫·休谟:"我自己的生活",大卫·菲特·诺顿编,《休谟剑桥指南》,剑桥:剑桥大学出版社,1993 年,第 352 页。

6 思想支脉

要点

- 休谟对神迹的描述持反对态度,同时他也反对"上帝是好的,所以有来生弥补今生的罪恶"这一观点。
- 休谟关于宗教的言论具有争议性。
- 他反对相信神迹的论点对宗教哲学和认识论影响巨大。

其他思想

在《人类理解研究》的最后几章,大卫·休谟总体上对宗教,尤其是对基督教,提出怀疑的论点,而1748年正值此书出版之际,基督教在欧洲占统治地位。尽管这些言论不是本书的主要观点,但之后被证明极具影响。

首先,休谟谈及神迹[1]。根据圣人传记和其他当代资料的记载,基督徒认为许多神迹发生在教会的早期历史中。但问题是这些记录是否可信。倘若可信的话,他们便为接受基督教提供了充分的理由。

然而休谟认为,这些传闻并不可信,因为它们无法用科学的方法证实。作为坚定的经验主义者,休谟认为只有当记述*,甚至是关于圣者的记述,与我们体验世界的一手经验一致时,才可被采信。休谟进一步指出,没有神迹,"任何理智的人都不会相信"[2]基督教,所以不得不对基督教本身的可信度产生怀疑。

其次,休谟发表了关于基督教完美力量和上帝的善意[3]的观点。他并未亲口说出内心的想法,而是利用文学的手法记录了他与朋友的一段对话。考虑到其观点的激进性和反传统的特性,休谟十分谨慎地不让别人将自己与观点中的结论联系在一起。基督徒相信，既然上帝尽善尽美且无所不能，我们有理由相信此世的不完美和邪恶将在后世得到补偿。休谟反对这个观点。

> "我们可以断言说，基督教不只在一开始时就带有许多神迹，但是即使现在，没有了神迹，任何具有理性思考能力的人都不会相信基督教。单纯的理性不足以使我们相信基督教的真实性；如果有人受了信条的鼓励来相信基督教，那他一定会亲身体验到有一个继续不断的神迹，这个神迹会推翻他的理解的一切原则，并且使他下决心相信与习惯和经验相反的事情。"
>
> —— 大卫·休谟：《宗教的自然史》

观点探究

依据休谟的定义，神迹不仅仅是不寻常或令人吃惊的事情。它是自然法则的暂停运行，这一刻，自然界中一直被视为真实的规律不再成立。因此，顾名思义，神迹是一种一直被人们认为不会发生的事情。在这种情况下，休谟指出，更合理的假设是神迹的证词是虚假的（无论是因为讲述者无知的错误，或是以误释曲解这一壮举，抑或是有意为之的欺骗），而非相信神迹确实发生了。

"没有证据都足以建构神迹，"休谟写道，"除非存在虚假的证据要比它所欲建立的那种事实更为神奇。"[4]

因循休谟的观点，也就是，所有的信念都应建立在经验证据之上，我们只能相信上帝强大和善良到证据能够表明其真实性的程度。举例来说，当基督徒假设无论我们是否能找到那个原因，世界上邪恶的存在一定是有原因的时候，他们犯了一个错误。与此类似，当他们认为，考虑到这个世界的不完美，就一定存在更美好的来世时，他们也犯了一个错误。秉承这些信念，休谟认为，基督教徒认为上帝比证据所证明的更完美的观点只是他们的假设。

在休谟的时代，这些观点十分激进并具原创性，极大地影响了后来者，他们努力使宗教信仰具有理性和基于证据的评价体系。休谟关于神迹的言说也在另一方面产生影响力，尤其在近代。这些言论成为证据认识论辩论时的经典文本，也就是，利用他人口头或书面词语作为知识的来源[5]。

被忽视之处

《人类理解研究》一书虽短，却被深入研究了长达两个多世纪。此书的每个部分都吸引了许多关注。然而，特别是直到最近，本书的某些方面相比之下仍然被忽视。其中之一就是休谟参与古希腊怀疑论传统的深度。怀疑论在哲学上常被视为一种挑战，其中，哲学家试图反驳怀疑论者，证明知识是可能的。但是休谟发现希腊传统中有另一种态度，即怀疑论也有指明如何生活，带来积极愿景的一面。

休谟指出，虽然我们的许多信念并不完全依赖理性，但它们是人类本性中非理性的产物，比如感情、动物本能以及期待。他并未将此看作是要纠正的问题。他承认，光凭理性不足以建立世界观，我们也绝不能仅依靠理性重建信仰体系。相反，休谟认为，我们要简单地接受很多信念中根本存在的非理性基础。这与古希腊哲学家皮浪*的追随者，即皮浪怀疑主义者，有异曲同工之处。皮浪怀疑论者认为既然人类自身并不能获得知识，因此我们应该停止对世界本身的方式做出判断，并遵循本能而非信念行动。

然而，休谟不同于古代的怀疑论者。在《人类理解研究》的结尾，他写道，"皮浪主义或是怀疑主义的过度原则作为伟大的颠覆者是对日常生活的行动、偏用和占有。"[6] 他认为，信念是人类的本性，倘若没有信念，个体将无法生活。休谟建议在日常生活背后抛开怀疑态度：不是因为这些怀疑未被证实，而是出于实际的意图或目的，我们必须忽视它们。

---

1. 大卫·休谟：《人类理解研究》，剑桥：剑桥大学出版社，2007年，第96-116页。
2. 休谟：《人类理解研究》，第116页。
3. 休谟：《人类理解研究》，第117-130页。
4. 休谟：《人类理解研究》，第101页。
5. 见《证据的认识论》中的散文，詹妮弗·莱基和欧内斯特·索莎编，牛津：牛津大学出版社，2006年。
6. 休谟：《人类理解研究》，第139-140页。

7 历史成就

要点

- 休谟的怀疑论观点,尤其是对因果和神迹信仰的论述,被广泛的研究和接受。
- 后世的哲学家经常在休谟的作品中为自己的课题找到灵感。
- 特别是自从18世纪末期德国哲学家伊曼努尔·康德的著作推出后,休谟就被解读为对知识提出了怀疑论的挑战。而他构想的人类思维理论这个更大的课题却常常被忽略。

观点评价

大卫·休谟在《人类理解研究》中对哲学和心理学都进行了探索。一方面,这本书与认识论有关。作为哲学家的休谟评估了我们关于知识的论断(例如,关于知识中的因果关系或是神迹的论断)。他对这些论断持广泛的怀疑态度,认为我们提出论断的理由并不充分。

另一方面,作为科学家的休谟提出了思维运作模式的心理学理论。他对解释思维为什么这么运作,以及我们为何信自己所信感兴趣。他对评估信念并不感兴趣,他希望解释信念。

有理由相信,休谟创作《人类理解研究》的主要目的在于提出关于思维的理论。这本书简要介绍了他在《人性论》中提出的观点,"尝试用实验的方法解释道德问题。"简而言之,《人性论》试图利用科学的推理方法研究人类。

休谟关于因果信念与神迹信仰的论点极具影响力。如今写这些话题的人都绕不开他的观点。事实上很多人都认为休谟的这些论点是完全正确的。例如，20世纪澳大利亚哲学家约翰·莱斯利·麦基*在他的经典之作《有神论的奇迹》[1]中讨论了这一点。自相矛盾的是，正是休谟认识论论证的成功和显著性导致人们忽略了他整体的心理学工程。对休谟而言，他在心理学上的论点比认识论（即关于知识的理论）方面的论点更为重要。但后者的影响更为深远。

> "大卫·休谟是最重要的哲学家之一，他发展了洛克和贝克莱的经验主义哲学，得出合乎逻辑的结论，使之自成体系，令人惊叹。在某种程度上，他呈现了一个死胡同：因循着他的研究方向，已经无法再深入走下去。"
>
> ——伯特兰·罗素：《西方哲学史》

当时的成就

19世纪及20世纪初期，许多评论家受德国哲学家伊曼努尔·康德的影响，将休谟首先看作是挑战我们对世界既定信念的怀疑论者。后休谟哲学家的作用在于致力于发现这些信念是否可以被用来为加在休谟身上的批评进行辩护。

但自20世纪中期，休谟开始普遍被看作是自然主义哲学家（这类哲学家相信只有自然法则才会影响万物的行为）。这种观点早期最具有影响力的拥护者是休谟的苏格兰同乡诺曼·坎普·史密斯，他是《大卫·休谟的哲学》一书的作者。[2]在这本书中，坎普·史密斯指出，休谟试图根据自然科学的准则研究人类思维，因此将人类看作是自然世界的一部分。

如果学者认为理解休谟的观点十分困难,一个很好的例子便是他关于因果关系的观点。休谟认为我们试图用因果关系解释事件间的联系的根本原因是我们思维的结构,而非观察的证据。但这引发了另一个有争议的问题:休谟仅仅在描述人类形成信念的过程还是对因果关系是否存在提出疑问?

许多年以来,休谟一直被视为对因果关系普通信念找到合理解释的富有挑战性的哲学家。但最近的书中出现一种具有替代作用的观点,非常流行,如英国分析哲学家盖伦·斯特劳森*的著作《隐秘连结》。其中阐释道,休谟并不质疑因果关系的存在,他总体上研究的是完全不同的话题,他对信念如何产生的心理学解释与信念正确与否没有任何关系。

局限性

对《人类理解研究》的解释随着时间的推移发生巨大的变化,从某些方面来看,不同的地方解释也发生变化。但人们对这本书的兴趣却从未消减;无论身处何地,不同时代的读者都能从这本书中发现有意义的内容。读者认为休谟的作品反映了他们自身的兴趣和观念。例如,20世纪早期的读者从中看到了逻辑经验主义或逻辑实证主义*的兴起,这些运动的主张与休谟的观点一致,认为只有经过科学证实的事实才是合理的。对逻辑实证主义者来说,休谟是先驱人物。之后,自然主义哲学家重新将休谟解读为哲学和科学处于同一体系中,并基本采用同一类方法。

欧洲大陆的哲学家所普及推广的观点不同于英国和北美的哲学家,因此他们对休谟作品的理解和其对学科的重要性都有所不同也就不足为奇了。德国现象学*学者爱德蒙·胡塞尔*在他的著作

《欧洲科学的危机》³ 中将休谟理解为通过贬低经验主义至荒谬的程度来显示"破产"的经验主义哲学家。休谟的观点展现了经验主义如何引起怀疑主义和唯我主义 *（唯我主义认为人唯一能确定了解的是自己。）：如果经验是知识的唯一来源，我们无法确定外部世界甚至他人是否存在。胡塞尔认为，休谟的作品展现了哲学新开端的必要性，以避免这些荒诞的结论。

在《经验主义与主体性》⁴ 一书中，法国哲学家吉尔·德勒兹 * 认为休谟是反基础论主义者（他们认为哲学不应该试图找到比我们自身和世界的直接经历更确信或基础的事物）的先驱者。德勒兹欣赏休谟对自我和知识的形而上基础（那里有什么以及它是什么样的？）的否定。

---

1. 约翰·莱斯利·麦基：《有神论的奇迹：支持与反对上帝的存在》，牛津：牛津大学出版社，1982年。
2. 诺曼·坎普·史密斯：《大卫·休谟的哲学》，伦敦：麦克米伦出版社，1941年。
3. 爱德蒙·胡塞尔，大卫·卡尔译：《欧洲科学的危机和超验论的现象学》，埃文斯顿：西北大学出版社，1970年。
4. 吉尔·德勒兹，康斯坦丁·瓦·邦达兹译：《经验主义与主体性》，纽约：哥伦比亚大学出版社，1991年。

8 著作地位

要点

- 休谟一生都努力构建关于人性的科学。
- 《人类理解研究》重申了休谟早期作品——三卷本的《人性论》中提到的观点。
- 休谟现在很大程度上是以《人类理解研究》和《人性论》(第一卷)而获得知名度。

定位

大卫·休谟发表《人类理解研究》之时已37岁,还未因写书而出名。据休谟自己所言,他在少年时便已形成自己的哲学思想,事实上,他在23岁时就开始撰写《人性论》,比《人类理解研究》早了十年,书中提出了很多《人类理解研究》中的论断以及理论。

《人性论》冗长艰涩。当它首次发表时,并没有很多读者。休谟希望更加简短易读的《人类理解研究》可以被更多的读者所接受。他如愿以偿,但却是在去世后。休谟生前最出名的著作是有关历史的创作以及深受大众欢迎的散文,而非其哲学作品。

休谟从未动摇过他的哲学体系中的根本实质,也从未更改过他的重要结论:无论是早期还是晚期,他都希望建立关于人性的科学用以系统地解释作为思维、感觉和行为的人类。《人性论》试图涵盖这个庞大领域的所有内容。在相对简短的《研究》中,休谟更聚焦于研究人类的理解,尤其将人看作信仰和认知的主体。他提出了我们为什么会相信我们所相信的一切这个问题。

> "没有任何在文学上的尝试比起《人性论》来说还要来得不幸。他从出版的那一天就死亡了。它是这样的无声无息,甚至连狂徒的任何闲言碎语都没有能够激起。"
>
> ——大卫·休谟:《我自己的生活》

整合

休谟在《人性论》和《人类理解研究》这两本书中得到的结论对他所有的哲学著作都十分重要。在他对人性的阐释中,理智的作用有限。在休谟看来,我们所思所做的大部分事情起因于本性,并不仅作为能够理性推理的存在,而是作为具备同理性毫无关系的情感、本能和期待的存在。

这个观点引起对某些信念的怀疑论,尤其是对宗教信仰的怀疑论:休谟对我们身体力行的宗教信仰提出质疑,认为我们是因为被言论和证据说服。休谟认为,一旦证据不存在了,宗教信仰就没有理由存在。但这个观点在 18 世纪极具争议性,事实上,这个观点时至今日也会在某些圈子中引发愤怒。因此休谟选择删除《人性论》中许多宗教观点。他晚年以论证反对信仰上帝,这个观点尤其体现在他最后一部著述《自然宗教对话录》中。这本书极具争议性,以至于休谟要求死后再出版此书。

休谟的另一个结论是情感的,或者休谟称其为"情绪"对精神生活的重要性。他因此而形成了对道德(对与错背后的准则)与美学(有关自然与美德的准则)的观点,他在其他作品,包括很受欢迎的《道德政治和文学论文集》中表达过此类观点。在 1757 年发表的重要论文"论品味的标准"一文中,休谟指出,当我们对美做出判断时,评判的标准基于感情而非客观事实。因此这些判断仅仅体现了做出判断的人的本性。[1]

意义

《人类理解研究》是休谟最重要且最具持久影响力的作品之一。《人类理解研究》与《人性论》的第一卷本有许多相似之处，休谟在其中对人类理解和知识提出了明确的观点。休谟同等重要的哲学论著是《人性论》的第二卷和第三卷，在这两本书中，他分别对情感和道德进行了阐述。

换句话说，奠定休谟西方重要哲学家地位的书籍主要有两本，即《人类理解研究》和《人性论》。

几乎《人类理解研究》的每一章节都引发激烈的哲学辩论。知识和怀疑论的章节被看作是认识论的经典文本。对神迹阐释的章节在宗教哲学中十分重要，正如对自由意志的论述对形而上学研究十分重要一样。也许最重要的是，对因果关系的探索产生了归纳法*，归纳法是科学哲学的核心问题。归纳法通过观察推导出普遍原理，通常被认为是科学发现的关键要素。

另一个激烈的辩论是关于如何正确地解读休谟。尽管他的表述清晰明了，但对其观点的意图方面仍有相当多的不同意见，不同时期的哲学家对休谟的解读大相径庭。

---

[1] 大卫·休谟：《道德、政治和文学论文集》，印第安纳波利斯：自由经典出版社，1985年。

第三部分：学术影响

9 最初反响

要点

- 评论家批判了休谟的理论观点和他的因果关系论述。
- 休谟反驳这些评论家相信"天赋观点",这无异于说他们是过时的思想家。
- 康德和其他哲学家认为休谟的哲学思想带来了怀疑论,如果要避开怀疑主义就要反对休谟的观点。

批评

休谟在世时,很少有哲学家阅读并对《人类理解研究》中的言论作出回应。作出回应的最重要的思想家是一位苏格兰哲学家托马斯·里德*,他在首版发表于1764年[1]的著作《按常识原理探究人类心灵》中提出了他的观点。

里德反对休谟哲学的基本观点(里德称其为"思想方式")。同时期的其他重要思想家,例如约翰·洛克和乔治·贝克莱,也持有此观点。根据休谟等其他支持思维方式的思想家的观点,我们永远不能直接感知并理解外部世界;相反,我们只能形成思维认知和观念。例如,当我看橘黄色的球,我的脑海里出现了圆形的橘黄色物体。我看到的是观念,而非实体。思维并没有直接与外部物体关联。

里德认为这个观点是错误的。在他看来,思维并不由观点构成(即,我们所看所想之物),而由行为组成,即看与听的行为。通常,我们所看所想之物以物质实体的形式存在于思维之外。所以,里德说，我直接感知到了橘黄色的球；这个球并没有通过思维或其他中介进入我的大脑。

休谟认为，人类对因果关系的信念仅基于天性中对规则的观察；里德则回应，这样的观察无法为判断因果关系提供合理的依据。通常情况下，我们可以观察到，白天之后是夜晚，但我们并不会认为夜晚是白天到来的原因。再者，有时我们观察到的是因果关系的个例。例如，假设我看到一只鸟在飞行中撞破了玻璃，便由此得出结论鸟类是玻璃破碎的原因，尽管我之前并未看到此类情形，以后也不一定会看到。在里德看来，不能通过自然中常被观测到的范式理解因果关系。

> "我坦率地承认，许多年前，休谟第一次使我从独断主义的迷梦中惊醒，并为我指明了在思辨哲学领域研究的完全不同的方向。"
>
> ——伊曼努尔·康德：《未来形而上学导论》

回应

很遗憾的是对之后的学者，休谟并没有经常回应个别哲学家的批评。他直白得驳斥一位批评家、诗人兼哲学家，詹姆斯·比蒂*，在一封写给出版商的信件中称其为"固执的蠢货。"

在私人通信中，休谟简短地回复了里德，里德的批评并没有给休谟留下深刻的印象。他指责里德相信天赋*观点，那些我们与生俱来的观点。这与经验主义完全不同——经验主义主张我们的观点来自感知经验。很少有人赞同天赋观点，尤其在英国，因此休谟使用这个词组相当于称里德为过时的思想家。但休谟可能误解了里德的观点。里德的观点至少有一部分是认为感知和思考与外部世界相关。例如，感知的物体并非观念而是世界上的事物，例如橘黄色的球。

也许我们可以通过再次思考因果关系来理解休谟的观点。里德指出，事物具有因果力量，但是他并不认为我们可以感知因果力量。那么我们的大脑如何理解因果关系的概念？休谟认为，既然它不来自于感知，那么便是内在的、天生的。

19世纪以及20世纪早期，哲学家普遍认为休谟赢得了这场争论。但是20世纪，里德的观点被重新评估。当今，许多哲学家既支持直接感知的观点也认为因果力真实存在。今天，公平来说，一些哲学家赞同休谟，另一些则认同里德。纵使经过数百年的争论，仍然未能达成统一意见。

冲突与共识

伊曼努尔·康德是休谟同时期的德国哲学家，他指出，在阅读休谟的作品时，"他从独断主义的迷梦中惊醒。"[2] 康德发现休谟的观点令人不安：他不同意这个观点却发现它具有力量，这个观点急需回应。康德后期的哲学思想在很大程度上可以看作是对休谟的回应。对康德来说，休谟已经很清晰得表达出，我们对因果的理解并不来自于经验。然而，科学表明，我们确实具备此类知识。因此，康德认为，我们对因果的理解必须不能基于经验，而应仅仅依赖理智。如果能看到休谟对这一论断的回应将非常有趣，但是当康德最终于1781年[3]发表其回应之作——《纯粹理性批判》之时，休谟已经过世了。

康德认为，休谟的著作强调了科学方法。科学用具体的例子证明普遍结论的有效性。例如，我们认为所有拥有心脏的动物都有肾脏，并通过检验我们能找到的每一个物种来证明这一假说的正确性。但是这样的检测远不够得到一个普遍结论，因为我们有可能会发现一个有心脏却没有肾脏的新物种，这种复杂的情况就是归纳。休谟的论述被认为说明了归纳推理无法建立科学结论。因此，哲学家认为要回应休谟的论点，他们要么必须说明科学方法不适应于归纳法，要么必须接受科学知识是不可能的事实。

---

1. 托马斯·里德：《按常识原理探究人类心灵》，帕克：宾夕法尼亚州立大学出版社，1997年。
2. 伊曼努尔·康德，盖里·哈特菲尔德译编：《未来形而上学导论》，剑桥：剑桥大学出版社，1997年，第10页。
3. 伊曼努尔·康德，保罗·盖耶和艾伦·伍德译：《纯粹理性批判》，剑桥：剑桥大学出版社，1997年。

10 后续争议

要点

- 休谟的《人类理解研究》激起了有关经验主义知识的可能性以及归纳法的合法性的长期辩论，即用具体的例子检测普遍结论的正确性。
- 书中的论点影响了许多哲学家，例如逻辑实证主义者驳斥形而上学*的观点，认为其是无意义的。
- 当代的自然主义哲学家从休谟的思想中受益良多。

应用与问题

19世纪和20世纪的哲学家阅读休谟的《人类理解研究》及其他作品后相信休谟展现了经验主义的局限性。休谟认为经验主义是正确的：我们对世界的所有信念依赖于感知经验。但是他也指出，感知经验能够证明的信念少之又少。如果经验主义是"正确的，"我们完全依赖经验进行理性推理，那么我们无法获得关于世界的普遍真理，也无法进一步理解自然的因果秩序，更别说超越自然世界发现上帝或永生的形而上学的真理。在休谟的作品中，归纳问题成为认识论，即对知识的哲学性研究，和科学的哲学的巨大挑战。

一些理论家，如19世纪英国哲学家、经济学家约翰·斯图尔特·密尔*回应休谟道，倘若能概述并认真得遵循一种科学方法，将会得到合理可信但不完全确定的结论[1]。

他们支持的归纳法是理性的，区分好与不好的科学，但并不完全靠得住。没人能肯定地说好的科学就是正确的科学。20世纪，哲学家卡尔·波普提出了一个更加激进的提议：科学根本不需要归纳法[2]。波普提出，科学家提出的普遍理论仅仅是推测而非基于证据。科学的严谨性仅在设计实验证明这些猜想时发挥作用。在波普看来，科学只在于用实验*推翻*假设，而非*建立*假设。

德国哲学家伊曼努尔·康德提出了另一个传统，是对休谟观点的不同回应。康德和其追随者认为，关于世界的知识不能仅仅依靠感知经验建立。相对应的，我们需要先验*准则，即，与经验无关的准则。例如，世界由因果关系掌控，这个知识在康德看来就是先验。

但如何证明先验准则？如何把它们与非理性信仰或偏见区分？尽管在这个观点上，问题变得非常复杂，康德认为（简单来说）先验准则只有应用在可能经验的领域时，才是合理的。可以确定的是，因果关系掌控我们能体验的所有的事，但是我们不能确定所有存在的事都是可被掌控的。

> "如果我们相信这些学派，那么当我们巡行各个图书馆时，将有如何大的破坏呢？如果手里拿的是神学书或是形而上学方面的书，让我们问一个问题，这其中有任何包含量或数的抽象推理么？没有。其中包含任何关于事实和存在的经验推论么？没有。那么我们就可以把它投在烈火里，因为它所包含的没有别的，只有诡辩和幻想。"
>
> ——休谟：《人类理解研究》

思想流派

康德的理论与休谟观点的另一个主要的演变影响有关。休谟引导许多哲学家去怀疑形而上学*，传统意义上形而上学研究现实的根本性质。但休谟强调关于世界的知识是如何的因我们的生物属性而受到限制。他的作品使许多思想家怀疑人是否能够获得形而上学的知识。20世纪反形而上学的思想者,尤其是逻辑实证主义哲学家,例如第二次世界大战*之前维也纳著名的哲学家鲁道夫·卡内普*,以及同时期英国哲学家阿尔弗雷德·朱尔斯·艾耶尔*,都极大地受到了休谟的影响,无论是直接或是通过康德[3]受其影响。

事实上,逻辑实证主义可以被看作是休谟观点的激进版本。休谟认为只有两件事情可以拓展知识,提高我们对世界的理解:首先是依赖观察和实验的科学中存在的经验主义;第二是数学。在休谟看来,形而上学和神学*不属于这两类,并不丰富我们的知识。逻辑实证主义哲学家进一步展开推理,认为这些学派本身毫无意义。按照逻辑实证主义哲学家的观点,形而上学者以及神学家无法发现世界的真理,他们简直是在胡说八道。诸如"神创造了世界"之类的言论,倘若无法被实验和观察证明就没有任何意义。

当代研究

当下的政治学者认识到潘恩的《常识》对休谟的影响经受住了20世纪中期逻辑实证主义的衰退,那一时期,他普遍被认为是哲学自然主义者*。自然主义者认为哲学家和科学家都参与理解自然世界的课题当中。自然主义者从休谟的作品中得到启发,认为他们的首要目的便是建立了解思维的科学,以这样的方法使人类更彻底地进入科学领域。

这个课题对自然主义哲学家很有意义。例如美国学者威拉德·冯·奥曼·蒯因*在其文章《自然主义知识论》[4]中指出,知识论,即对知识的哲学研究,应被重新审视,将之纳入心理学的一部分。

对知识感兴趣的哲学家需利用科学方法研究人类如何产生知识。这便包含了研究思维实际上是如何运转的（例如，感知如何产生信念）。蒯因承认其自然主义知识论与休谟的精神一脉相承。近代哲学家，诸如阿尔文·戈德曼*发展了这一理论。

更广泛地说，近代哲学开始将人类思维看作是自然的一部分，与自然界的其他物体一样遵循法则，且能够用同样的方式进行解释。这个观点与休谟的观点一脉相承。

---

1. 约翰·斯图尔特·密尔：《逻辑学体系》，伦敦：约翰·帕克出版社，1843年。
2. 卡尔·波普：《猜测与反驳》，伦敦：劳特利奇出版社，2002年，第60页。
3. 阿尔弗雷德·朱尔斯·艾耶尔：《语言、真相与逻辑》，伦敦：格兰兹出版社，1946年；艾耶尔编：《逻辑实证主义》纽约：自由出版社，1959年。
4. 威拉德·冯·奥曼·蒯因："自然主义知识论"，《本体论的相对性及其他散文集》，纽约：哥伦比亚大学出版社，1969年。

11 当代印迹

要点 🗝

- 《人类理解研究》是探寻经验知识局限性的经典著作。
- 《人类理解研究》挑战了经验可以提供足够知识的观点,也挑战了我们可以拥有必然真理的知识的观点,除非那些知识太琐碎。
- 哲学家尝试缩小休谟观点中经验和理论的差距。

地位

大卫·休谟的著作,尤其是他在《人类理解研究》中的观点对现代思想论争所呈现的挑战来自于他严格的经验主义。经验主义认为,我们的知识来自于经验。如果信念超越了经验,我们只能进行猜想;这是我们不可知的事物。经验主义会带来某种怀疑主义(即,否认我们可以获得各种类型的知识)。尽管很多哲学家赞同经验主义,很少有人像休谟一样潜心研究它。

《人类理解研究》成为哲学经典著作,部分原因是它提出了挑战却迄今为止仍未得到回答。它挑战了经验主义传统中的观点,认为经验无法为我们对世界的信念提供合适的基础。哲学家用不同的方式回应这个挑战。其中,20世纪美国哲学家威拉德·冯·奥曼·蒯因赞同休谟的观点,反对为知识提供基础这一说法。其他哲学家,例如南非哲学家约翰·麦克道尔*,认为休谟指出了经验主义中经验这一概念是不充分的。在他们看来,感知经验比休谟的观点内涵更加丰富。他们确信,适当拓展经验这一概念,能够为知识提供基础。

> "我并不认为休谟留给我们的问题得到了很好的解决。休谟的困境是全人类的困境。"
> ——威拉德·冯·奥曼·蒯因:"自然主义知识论"

互动

休谟主义者在因果关系的问题上持怀疑论态度。许多人顺理成章地认为一件事导致另外一件事,或事物具有因果力。我们看到了一个球撞击玻璃,玻璃破碎,便认为球的冲击力导致了玻璃的破碎。休谟怀疑主义质疑我们是否应该这么想:我们所有经历的事件都是接连发生。我们不能将因果关系归结于自然的力量。

此外,休谟主义者认为,我们无法获知必然真理*(除非非常琐碎的知识)。休谟区分了他所说的"实际的真相"与"观念的连结"。在他看来,所有关于经验世界、自然世界的都是实际的真理。而观念的连结与我们自身概念相关。

数学提供了观念的连结:2 加 2 必等于 4;其他答案都是错误的。观念的连结的非数学例子是单身汉和未婚之间的联系。必要事实是单身汉都没有结婚,已婚人士不能被称为单身汉。但是休谟指出,这样的真理只能说明"单身汉"这一个概念,并不能说明真实世界。

这挑战了那些将自己看作探索世界必然真理的哲学家——形而上学背后的传统概念。特殊的科学,例如物理和生物,发现世界的真相具有偶然性;另一方面,普遍和必要事实属于形而上学的领域。休谟主义者怀疑是否存在这样的事实需要进行形而上学研究,他们相信,即使这样的事实真的存在,我们也无法获得具体的知识。

持续争议

休谟否认感知经验自身能够产生有关世界的知识。受德国哲学家伊曼努尔·康德的影响，一些思想家回应认为感知比休谟所说的更加丰富，能够产生更多的知识。当代这一观点的著名的倡导者是约翰·麦克道尔，在其著作《心灵和世界》[1]中认为感知经验在概念上十分丰富。在他看来，人类拥有的感知经验依赖于概念能力。例如，不同人对狗有不同的看法，因为我们对狗的背景知识是不同的。

休谟有一个重要论断，即经验事实——通过观察和实验得来的事实——不是必然真理，因为必然真理不能从逻辑上被否定。例如，数学事实似乎是必然真理的：只有 2 加 2 等于 4 是正确的，别的答案都不对。休谟认为可以用先验获得数学事实，用自己的逻辑推论，无需参考经验。通过经验发现的事实只能是偶然真理*；我们本质上对必要性的信念——例如，因果关系的必要性——不能仅仅通过经验研究就认为是正确的。

在近几十年最重要的哲学著作之一《命名与必然性》[2]一书中，美国分析哲学家索尔·克里普克*反对休谟主义的论断。克里普克认为，一些必然真理是经验的，科学家已经证实了这一真理。例如，克里普克认为，水由氢气和氧气组成的，这是必然真理，任何除此以外的组合都不是水。但是化学家要进行大量实验来验证这个真理。克里普克在重塑形而上学在哲学的中心位置的过程中发挥着巨大的作用。

麦克道尔和克里普克试图用不同的方式缩小休谟观点中经验和理论的差距，帮助证明信念——包括我们对因果关系和必然真理的信念——有时可以通过经验来证明。

1. 约翰·麦克道尔:《心灵和世界》,剑桥,马萨诸塞州:哈佛大学出版社,1996年。
2. 索尔·克里普克:《命名与必然性》,牛津:布莱克威尔出版社,1980年。

12 未来展望

要点

- 《人类理解研究》中讨论的话题,包括因果关系的本质和思维的本质,在哲学和心理学领域仍具有争议。
- 当代著名的思想家们继续发展休谟的观点试图解决这些问题。
- 《人类理解研究》是经验主义、自然主义以及怀疑主义发展中的重要文本。

潜力

《人类理解研究》出版200年后,哲学家和心理学家仍在讨论这本书中的诸多论断。其中一个论断与因果关系的本质有关:因果关系的法则仅仅是范式还是在本质上具有规律性?或者,因果关系而非真实力量是范式保持的原因?例如,吸烟引发癌症的说法。这是在说吸烟的人会更容易罹患癌症?还是说吸烟自身会带来癌症?

第二个辩论的议题是思维的本质。像其他的经验主义者一样,休谟相信思维中的所有内容都来自经验。当前的讨论大多围绕着概念问题(即,我们用以理解世界的总类)展开。例如,当我将餐具分为刀、叉和勺的时候,我运用了三种概念将餐具抽屉整理好。接下来的问题就是:我从哪里获得这些概念?它们都来自于经验么?或者,一些或所有的概念源自于其他来源,例如遗传基因?

> "(休谟)在哲学领域的权威严地位来自于其观点明晰,一次又一次地,他清晰地看出了我们的处境如何。"
>
> ——西蒙·布莱克本*:《如何解读休谟》

未来方向

许多当代哲学家遵从或重复休谟提出的观点。一群人数较少，但也可观的哲学家的著作深受休谟的影响，他们被称为"休谟主义者"。

其中一位思想家是英国哲学家海伦·毕比*，她是一位研究休谟著作的学者，其原创性哲学著作，尤其是在形而上学领域的著作，体现了休谟的影响力。毕比为休谟自然法则的概念辩护，即科学发现的关于宇宙的普遍法则。她认为，这些法则不能统治自然。他们仅仅能描述非常宽泛的自然范式，[1]无法决定宇宙将会发生什么。毕比认为，从更广的范围讲，自然界中没有必然：所有事物，包括自然科学可观察和可研究的事物，都仅仅是偶然。

如果毕比支持休谟的形而上学，美国哲学家杰西·普林茨*则支持休谟的思维哲学。在他的著作《装饰心灵》[2]中，普林茨认为我们的概念来自于感知经验。这便是经验主义，这个教义自休谟的时代便不断被抨击。但是，普林茨以现代心理学和认知科学（研究思维和思维的过程的科学）为依据，为经验主义进行复杂的辩护。普林茨认为，21世纪的科学很大程度上支持了休谟18世纪的世界观。

小结

毫无疑问，大卫·休谟的《人类理解研究》在西方哲学的伟大书籍中占有一席之地。尽管书很短，但它在许多不同话题方面引起了深刻的哲学讨论，并引发了不同流派的思考。

本书的部分影响来自休谟探寻经验主义的坚定和全力以赴。像其他经验主义者一样，休谟认为思维的所有内容来自感觉。但是休谟得出的结论是之前的经验主义者未曾发现的。例如，他的《人类理解研究》将因果关系的问题置于哲学讨论的中心，对本质上是否可以观察因果力提出意义深远的质疑。休谟认为，本质上来看，我们所能观察到的是具有规律性的重复的范式。

自休谟以来，哲学家对什么是因果关系产生疑惑，以及除了自然规律外是否还有什么别的概念。休谟对传统宗教信仰也产生了怀疑，他质疑在经验主义基础上，神迹信仰是否站得住脚。

倘若《人类理解研究》是经验主义传统的顶峰，它也是另一哲学传统——自然主义富有开创性的著作。

休谟运用其他自然领域科学研究的方法，对人类思维展开科学调查。倘若这样的方法成功，将会证明人是自然世界的一部分，与非人类的生物没有任何不同；人类拥有独特的特点，但是本质与自然界其他生物并无不同。20世纪，自然主义哲学家取得巨大进步，尽管许多当代自然主义的观点与休谟大相径庭，却和他的精神一脉相承。

《人类理解研究》对怀疑主义的当代探讨影响巨大。自17世纪勒内·笛卡尔出版其主要著作后，怀疑主义成为认识论中富有争议性的议题。笛卡尔与其假想的持怀疑主义态度的对手辩论，旨在说明能够获得关于世界的真知。

尽管哲学家对笛卡尔是否成功地反驳了怀疑论的观点众说纷纭，但休谟的论述与其他的论断有所不同，他指出了怀疑主义在智力层面上永远不可能回答问题的可能性：既然我们无法反驳怀疑论者，那么我们该如何生存？

---

1. 海伦·毕比："自然法则的非政府概念"，《哲学和现象学研究》第56卷，2000年：第571-594页
2. 杰西·普林茨：《装饰心灵：概念及其感知基础》，剑桥：麻省理工大学出版社，2002年。

术语表

1. **先验**：先验知识是与经验无关的知识。

2. **苏格兰教会**：苏格兰新教教会。

3. **偶然真理**：事情是真的但却不被要求是真的。"偶然真理"的对立面是"必然真理"。例如,德国的首都是柏林,但这个事实并不是必然真理,也可以将波恩设为首都。

4. **经验主义**：所有人类知识都来自于经验的观点。

5. **认识论**：知识的哲学研究。

6. **唯心主义**：认为没有现实可独立于思维而存在的观点。

7. **观点**：依据休谟的思维理论,观点是感知经验在大脑中产生的复制品。例如,我们关于黄色的概念便是从黄色物品的视觉体验中复制而来的。

8. **印象**：依据休谟的思维理论,印象是感知体验。大脑的其他内容、观念,都是印象的复制品。

9. **归纳法**：通过具体的例子推导出普遍理论的过程。

10. **天赋**：天生的特性指的是人与生俱来的特性,与习得的特性相对。

11. **逻辑实证主义**：激进的哲学运动,强调对语言的逻辑分析。逻辑实证主义者在20世纪20年代末期十分活跃,尤其在奥地利和德国。

12. **实际的真相**：与世界存在的方式有关。对休谟来说,观察和实验的结果才是实际的真相。

13. **形而上学**：哲学的一个领域,试图解释存在的本质和周围的世界。

14. **神迹**：与神或超自然原因有关的非凡的事件。

15. **自然主义**：哲学上，自然主义认为哲学与科学研究同一个课题，从本质上来讲，采取的方法也相同。

16. **必然真理**：不同于偶然真理，必然真理没有其他的可能。例如，单身汉都没有结婚是必然真理，不存在单身汉结婚的情况。

17. **现象学**：研究世界以何种方式呈现在人们面前的科学。

18. **现实主义**：认为世界与思维无关的观点。

19. **观念的连结**：对休谟来说，观念的连结与实际真相不同，它们与经验无关且十分确定。观念的连结包含数学真理。

20. **怀疑主义**：关于世界的真正知识是不存在的观点。

21. **苏格兰启蒙运动**：历史学家将18世纪苏格兰科学、哲学和文学鼎盛发展的时期称为苏格兰启蒙运动时期。

22. **唯我论，唯我主义**：认为他人并不存在。每个唯我主义者都认为他或她是唯一存在的人。

23. **诡辩术**：一门艺术，旨在产生表面上看似可信实则没有说服力的论断。

24. **记述**：通过言说或书写将知识从一个人传达给另一个人。

25. **神学**：研究神和宗教信仰的科学。

26. **第二次世界大战（1939-1945）**：许多国家都参与的全球性战争，彼时的超级大国全部参战。

人名表

1. 阿尔弗雷德·朱尔斯·艾耶尔（1901-1989），英国哲学家，以在英国和美国普及逻辑实证主义而闻名。

2. 皮埃尔·贝尔（1647-1706），法国哲学家和散文家，强调人类理性的局限性以及获得某些知识的不可能性。

3. 詹姆斯·比蒂（1735-1803），苏格兰诗人和哲学家，因其道德哲学领域的著作而闻名。

4. 海伦·毕比，英国哲学家，其关于形而上学和休谟的著作十分出名。

5. 乔治·贝克莱（1685-1753），爱尔兰哲学家，他主张经验主义和理想主义。

6. 西蒙·布莱克本（1944出生），英国哲学家，尝试普及学科的概念。

7. 罗伯特·波义耳（1627-1691），爱尔兰科学家，化学的奠基人，17世纪最重要科学家之一。

8. 鲁道夫·卡内普（1891-1970），德国哲学家，逻辑实证主义运动的领袖。他对逻辑学、语言哲学和科学哲学都做出了巨大贡献。

9. 塞缪尔·克拉克（1675-1729），英国哲学家和神学家，他为艾萨克·牛顿的哲学观点辩护，他认为上帝存在。

10. 吉尔·德勒兹（1925-1995），法国哲学家，以其在形而上学和艺术哲学领域的著作而闻名。

11. 勒内·笛卡尔（1596-1650），法国科学家、数学家、哲学家，被看作是现代最重要的哲学家之一。

12. 阿尔文·戈德曼（1938出生），美国哲学家，以其认识论的著作而闻名。

13. 爱德蒙·胡塞尔（1859-1938），德国哲学家，被认为是现象学的奠基人（研究经验和意识的结构的学科）。

14. 弗朗西斯·哈奇森（1694-1746），苏格兰哲学家，以其道德哲学和情感理论而闻名。

15. 詹姆斯·哈顿（1726-1797），苏格兰科学家，被看作是现代地质学的奠基人。

16. 伊曼努尔·康德（1724-1804），德国哲学家，著有《纯粹理性批判》一书（1781年）。他被看作是现代最具影响力的哲学家。

17. 索尔·克里普克（1940出生），美国哲学家，对逻辑学、语言哲学和其他诸多领域都贡献巨大。普遍认为，克里普克是当代最重要的哲学家之一。

18. 约翰·洛克（1632-1704），英国哲学家，以对认识论、思维哲学和政治哲学的贡献而出名。

19. 约翰·莱斯利·麦基（1917-1981），澳大利亚哲学家，对伦理学、形而上学以及宗教哲学的发展有贡献。

20. 约翰·麦克道尔（1942出生），英国哲学家，其著作涉及领域众多，涵盖亚里士多德哲学、伦理学、认识论以及思维哲学。

21. 约翰·斯图尔特·密尔（1806-1873），英国哲学家，以其对科学哲学、伦理学以及政治哲学领域的贡献而闻名。

22. 艾萨克·牛顿（1642-1727），英国科学家、数学家和哲学家。他常被看作是历史上最伟大的物理学家和数学家之一。

23. 卡尔·波普（1902-1994），澳大利亚哲学家。他也许是20世纪最著名的科学哲学家之一。

24. 杰西·普林茨，美国哲学家、认知科学家，其心理学、情感和美学方面的创作既面向学术领域也面向普罗大众。

25. 埃利斯的皮浪（公元前360-270），古希腊哲学家。尽管他从未著书,但被看作是激进的怀疑论者。他相信知识是不可能的,人类不应该尝试获得有关世界的知识。

26. 威拉德·冯·奥曼·蒯因(1908-2000),美国哲学家,对逻辑学、语言哲学、认识论和科学哲学领域的发展均有贡献。

27. 托马斯·里德(1710-1769),苏格兰哲学家,以知觉论而著名。

28. 塞克斯都·恩披里克(公元前160-210),希腊物理学家,最著名的是其关于认识论的著作,这本书体现了他赞同怀疑主义的观点。

29. 亚当·斯密(1723-1790),苏格兰哲学家、经济学家,被看作是现代经济学的奠基人之一。

30. 詹姆斯·圣·克莱尔(1688-1762),苏格兰士兵、政治家。

31. 盖伦·斯特劳森(1952出生),英国哲学家,在形而上学、思维哲学和哲学历史领域都发表著作。

32. 詹姆斯·瓦特(1736-1819),苏格兰工程师,发明了现代蒸汽机。

WAYS IN TO THE TEXT

KEY POINTS

- David Hume (1711–76) was a Scottish philosopher.
- Published in 1748, Hume's *An Enquiry Concerning Human Understanding* is an account of the origins of our beliefs about the world.
- It is one of the greatest works of the British empiricist* tradition in philosophy.

Who Was David Hume?

David Hume was born in the Scottish city of Edinburgh in 1711 to an aristocratic, if not very wealthy, family. A scholarly young man, Hume entered the University of Edinburgh at the age of 12. He left without a degree, however, and could not get a position at a university in later years—partly because of his religious views. Hume did not accept Christianity. Indeed, he arguably did not believe in God at all, and as the Church of Scotland* controlled Scottish universities, someone with his religious views would not have been seen as a model employee.

He became a diplomat and a writer instead. Soon, many saw him as a leading figure in the Scottish Enlightenment,* a period during which science and literature flourished in Scotland. Hume knew many leading intellectuals in Edinburgh, London and Paris, and spent time in rural France working on his philosophical writings. His first published work, *A Treatise of Human Nature*, in which he presented his theory of the human mind, appeared in 1738. Its sales were slow at first, so Hume wrote a shorter, more popular introduction to his ideas—*An Enquiry Concerning Human*

Understanding. In 1754 he gained fame as the author of the hugely popular *History of England*.

In his later years, Hume wrote a book arguing against belief in God. It was published as *Dialogues Concerning Natural Religion* after his death in Edinburgh in 1776; the book's subject was considered so highly controversial that Hume chose to publish it posthumously.

Although many think Hume was the greatest philosopher ever to write in English, he was best known during his lifetime as a historian. He was the last great figure in the philosophical movement called British empiricism, which emphasized the importance of experience in human thought and knowledge.

What Does *An Enquiry Concerning Human Understanding* Say?

Through his philosophy, Hume attempted to understand something that science had not yet explained: the workings of the human mind. While contemporary science had made great progress in understanding the world, the mind still remained largely unexplored. Hume set out to change that, using scientific principles to explore the ways we think about the act of thinking.

In Hume's view, many of our beliefs about the world stem neither from experience nor reason but from the way our minds work. In short, we have the beliefs we do because of human nature.

Hume begins his argument with an empiricist principle that everything in the mind is either an impression* or an idea.* By "impression" he means, roughly, a sense experience. An "idea" is a copy of an impression. Suppose, for example, that you see a red apple. In seeing the apple you gain an impression of it. But when you call it to mind, even just a moment later, what you remember is an idea copied from the impression.

Hume points out that we make sense of our experience by believing that one thing causes another. But our belief in this idea of what is called "causation" does not itself derive from any experience; according to Hume, it comes from certain habits of mind. We are in the habit of expecting the future to be like the past, for example. But this habit is not justified by experience; we create it because it is our human nature to do so.

This lead Hume to the issue of skepticism,* the school of philosophy that believes true knowledge is impossible. If our beliefs about the world do not come from experience, Hume argues, then why would we have those beliefs? Can we know anything about the world? According to Hume, philosophical reasoning suggests we cannot. But people need to form beliefs about the world in order to live their lives. Belief in causation—one thing causing another—is too central to human nature to be undermined by a philosophical argument.

Hume was influenced by previous philosophers, especially the British empiricist John Locke.* Locke believed that sense experiences—thoughts, perceptions or emotions—produce ideas, and we hold those ideas in the mind. We cannot know a color, for example, unless we have seen it. In Locke's view, we can understand everything in the mind, including beliefs, by asking what experiences caused them.

Later philosophers like Immanuel Kant* saw Hume as pushing empiricism to its logical conclusion: if empiricism is a valid method of understanding things, if every idea must be tested and verified scientifically, then we cannot have any genuine knowledge of the world. These philosophers saw Hume as unintentionally demonstrating that empiricism cannot be valid because its logical conclusion is skepticism, and skepticism is absurd because there are things one can know with certainty. I know my name, for example, and that London is the capital of Britain. In the mid-twentieth century, the philosopher Bertrand Russell noted that Hume's philosophical reasoning leads to "a dead end; in his direction, it is impossible to go further."

More recent students of Hume have interpreted him differently, and understand him as not showing that knowledge is either possible or impossible at all. According to them, Hume is, in fact, practicing psychology, showing how the mind works. Hume does not ask whether our beliefs are true or false. He asks, rather, why we have them and where they come from.[1]

Why Does *An Enquiry Concerning Human Understanding* Matter?

Hume's arguments resonate throughout subsequent thinking in philosophy, psychology and science. Their historical importance cannot be denied.

The history of psychology sees Hume's arguments as pioneering attempts to understand the human mind by using scientific methods. Although later psychologists adopted more complex models of the mind, Hume's theory of the mind was an influential early attempt.

In the discipline of philosophy, Hume contributed to epistemology,* or the study of knowledge. He asked how it was possible for human beings to gain knowledge and showed that our beliefs about the world are less secure than we would like to think—experience alone cannot account for them.

Hume also challenged belief in the existence of God, arguing that we have no good reason to believe that God exists or that miracles* occur. These are fundamental issues, still being debated.

Today, we often see science as the best way to understand the world and advance knowledge. Hume would agree—he was an early advocate of the scientific world view. But we think of science as based on evidence; Hume challenges that assumption. For him, evidence alone cannot account for scientific beliefs—there is always a gap between the evidence and scientific claims. Philosophers and scientists who want to understand science itself must confront Hume's arguments.

More generally, Hume's approach offers a good way to challenge our own beliefs about the world. Hume always asks where our beliefs come from and why we hold them. He looks for the roots of our beliefs in our experience of the world. He teaches us a critical method that can be applied to every belief. Even if we disagree with Hume's conclusions, we can use his methods to test our beliefs.

Hume's *Enquiry* is also a beautifully written book, well worth reading just for his prose style. It is clear evidence of the reason many regard Hume as one of the greatest philosophical writers.

---

1. Bertrand Russell, *History of Western Philosophy* (London: Routledge, 2004), 600.

SECTION 1
INFLUENCES

MODULE 1
THE AUTHOR AND THE HISTORICAL CONTEXT

KEY POINTS

- *An Enquiry Concerning Human Understanding* is one of the most influential books ever written on the workings of the human mind.
- Hume came from a devout Christian background, but turned his back on religion when he was a young man to study philosophy, especially as it relates to the mind.
- He wrote during a period of great intellectual development known as the Scottish Enlightenment.*

Why Read this Text?

Many people regard David Hume's *An Enquiry Concerning Human Understanding*, published in 1748, as the best example of the British empiricist* tradition in philosophy. Empiricism is the view that all human knowledge comes from experience. Empiricists believed everything that exists in the mind comes from our senses; Hume traces the contents of the mind, and especially a person's beliefs, back to their roots in the experience of the senses.

Hume's conclusion aligns with skeptical* philosophy: the view that genuine knowledge of the world is impossible to attain. In Hume's opinion, experience cannot be the reason behind our beliefs about the world. Rather, the experiences we have result to a large degree from certain habits of mind. These habits may explain our beliefs, but do not provide a rational reason for them. Hume thinks we cannot help but have these beliefs because practical life would be impossible without them.

This argument is important both to the philosophy of the mind and to the field of psychology. Hume offered a naturalistic* account of the mind. In philosophy, naturalism is the view that philosophy and science are both trying to understand life as it really is. When Hume was writing in the middle of the eighteenth century, scientists like Isaac Newton* had already made great progress in understanding the physical world. Hume hoped to extend this progress to the mind by applying scientific methods to its study.

Second, Hume's skeptical conclusions are important in epistemology,* the philosophical study of knowledge. Some commentators say that Hume's work shows that empiricism leads to absurd conclusions (specifically, the conclusion that we have no knowledge of causal relations—that is, the fact that one thing causes another). By arguing that all knowledge depends on sense experience, Hume unintentionally (these commentators believed) showed that empiricism must be false. The most important thinker to hold this view was the German philosopher Immanuel Kant,* whose work attempted to explain the relationship between the way people reason and the things they experience. Other people believe that Hume's skepticism reveals a fundamental problem facing human knowledge: that genuine knowledge of the world is impossible. The Austrian philosopher Karl Popper* was an important supporter of this view in the twentieth century.[1]

> "I found a certain boldness of temper growing in me, which was not inclined to submit to any authority in these subjects, but led me to seek out some new medium, by which truth might be established. After much study and reflection on this, at last, when I was about 18 years of age, there seemed to be opened up to me a new scene of thought, which transported me beyond measure, and made me, with an ardor natural to young men, throw up every other pleasure or business to apply entirely to it."
>
> —— David Hume, *A Kind of History of My Life*

Author's Life

Hume was born into the minor Scottish gentry in Edinburgh in 1711. His parents, though comfortably off, were not particularly rich, so Hume was never able to live off the family estate; he had to work for a living. Educated at home by tutors, Hume became a voracious reader at a very young age. He went to the University of Edinburgh at just 12 years of age (most people started at 14) and studied there for four years, though he did not receive a degree.[2]

Hume decided to make his way in the world as an independent scholar. In later life he applied for academic positions at the University of Edinburgh and the University of Glasgow, but was turned down for both. This could be because his views about religion, mainly his doubts as to the existence of God, were regarded as unorthodox and dangerous.

Hume's first major work, *A Treatise of Human Nature*,[3] was published in three volumes in 1739 and 1740. A long book that failed to find many readers at first or make much of an impression on scholars, Hume famously said the *Treatise* "fell dead-born from the press."4

In an effort to attract a wider audience for his ideas, Hume published the shorter and more accessible *An Enquiry into Human Understanding* in 1748. By this time he was working as secretary to the Scottish soldier and politician Lieutenant-General James St Clair.* Hume became involved in politics and diplomacy himself, work that took him to great European cities like Vienna and Turin. He had many friends in intellectual circles in Edinburgh, in London and in France, where he lived for a time.5

Hume's six-volume *History of England* was published between 1754 and 1762 and became a bestseller, bringing him wealth and fame as a historian rather than as a philosopher. He died of a form of abdominal cancer in the city of his birth, Edinburgh, at the age of 65 in 1776.

Author's Background

The mid-eighteenth century in Hume's native Scotland was a time of great intellectual progress in science, philosophy and literature—so much so that the period has become known as the Scottish Enlightenment. Important figures of the time included the economist Adam Smith* (a personal friend of Hume's), the scientist James Hutton,* and James Watt,* who invented the modern steam engine. Moving in these circles, Hume lived and wrote in a cultured and open intellectual environment independent of the universities and religious authorities.

Like most Scots of the time, Hume's family practiced a strict and rigid form of Christianity. Hume himself said he was a religious child who took the teachings of Christianity very seriously. But while at university he read many philosophical and scientific works and seems to have abandoned religion. At the end of his life, Hume said that he had never truly believed in religion after reading the English philosophers John Locke* and Samuel Clarke.*6 In his philosophical writings, Hume seems suspicious of religion in general and of Christianity in particular.

Because of his beliefs, some members of the clergy saw Hume as a radical. In this they were not wrong. Knowing that his views would displease some authorities and unwilling to risk having his entire body of work censored, Hume insisted that his last important philosophical writings, a discussion about religion and the existence of God, should not be published in his lifetime. *Dialogues Concerning Natural Religion*7 appeared in 1779, three years after he died.

---

1. Karl Popper, Conjectures and Refutations (London: Routledge, 2002), 55–61.
2. David Hume, "My Own Life," in The Cambridge Companion to Hume, ed. David Fate Norton (Cambridge: Cambridge University Press, 1993), 351.
3. Hume, A Treatise of Human Nature (Oxford: Oxford University Press, 1978).
4. Hume, "My Own Life," 352.
5. Hume, "My Own Life," 352–3.
6. James Boswell, "An account of my last interview with David Hume, Esq," in Boswell in Extremes 1776–1778, ed. Charles Weis and Frederick Pottle (New York: McGraw-Hill, 1970), 11.
7. Hume, Dialogues Concerning Natural Religion (Cambridge: Cambridge University Press, 2007).

MODULE 2
ACADEMIC CONTEXT

KEY POINTS

- Sir Isaac Newton* and other scientists transformed our understanding of the natural world in the seventeenth century.
- Philosophers and scientists aimed to use the methods of the new science to understand the human mind.
- Hume was influenced both by these efforts and by the ancient skeptical* tradition that had been revived by Pierre Bayle.*

The Work In Its Context

David Hume's *An Enquiry Concerning Human Understanding* capitalized on advances in natural science made by his predecessors in the seventeenth and eighteenth centuries. Isaac Newton's* system of physics, first published in 1687, set out a new conception of the physical world, heavily mathematical but based on rigorous empirical* (that is, evidence-based) testing. The new science launched a revolution in both methods and theories, using experiment and observation to test its results. It also described the world using very general principles, which it used to explain phenomena that had previously seemed very varied. Newton's law of universal gravitation, for example, explained both the motion of objects on the surface of the earth and the movements of the planets.

Thinkers of this era drew no clear distinctions between philosophy and science. The two were considered as a single discipline, divided into "natural philosophy"—the study of the natural world, including physics, astronomy, chemistry and biology—and "moral philosophy," which concerned itself more specifically with human beings.

In the hands of scientists like Newton and Robert Boyle,* who is today generally recognized as one of the first practitioners of modern chemistry, the new scientific method had achieved great results in natural philosophy. But it had not yet been applied in a sustained way to moral philosophy. Scholars began to dream of extending the new methods into the domain of human society and economics, and of human psychology.

> "[Hume's work] aimed at no less than the destruction of the doctrine of the image of God, and substituted for it an anthropology which looked not to the divine but to the natural world for its comparisons, and to the sciences for its methods. Man was a natural object; not, as for Leibniz, a little god beside the great God, but a great animal among the lesser animals."
> —— Edward Craig, *The Mind of God and the Works of Man*

Overview of the Field

The desire to study thought has a long history—perhaps as long as the history of thoughts themselves. In the seventeenth century, the French philosopher René Descartes* theorized about "the way of ideas." According to Descartes and his followers, "ideas" occur in our minds when we think, feel or perceive something. Introspection—the examination of our own mental processes—

gives us direct access to those ideas. When I see a green patch of grass for example, or merely imagine or think of a green patch, I get an idea of greenness.

A century later, British empiricism* added to the mix the notion of applying newly expressed scientific principles to the study of the human mind. The empiricists believed that the contents of the mind come from sense experience; to them, ideas were mental representations of the outside world that arrive in the mind through the sense organs. Hume's most important influences in this tradition were the English philosopher John Locke* and the Irish philosopher George Berkeley.*

In tracing ideas back to sense experiences, Locke argued that the world is very different from our common-sense conception of it and that we can only discover the true nature of the world through natural science. Berkeley came to an even more radical conclusion, arguing that there is no material world at all: nothing exists except ideas and the minds in which ideas occur, including the mind of God.

Academic Influences

Hume was a keen reader of Descartes, Locke, Berkeley and the other philosophers who had contributed to the growing debate about the mind. But he was also influenced by other intellectual trends in his time, like the revival of interest in an ancient Greek school of thought called Pyrrhonian skepticism.* This tradition was repopularized by the French philosopher Pierre Bayle,* who gained fame with a book of essays called the *Historical and Critical*

Dictionary (1697), a work Hume often mentioned.

Pyrrhonian skeptics thought that truth was not accessible to human beings: Since we are always liable to error, we should suspend judgment. Instead of trying to find out about the world, skeptics believed that we should just live according to our natural instincts.

Bayle popularized skepticism, but not by putting forward a general principle that knowledge is impossible. Instead, he examined many different systems of belief, including religious beliefs—finding each uncertain and open to doubt. In this way Bayle emphasized the limitations of human reason. Bayle concluded, among other things, that since the human mind is always liable to make mistakes, we should tolerate different opinions. In particular, he argued, we should not persecute other people's religions.

MODULE 3
THE PROBLEM

KEY POINTS

- Philosophers and scientists asked how the mind worked; in particular, where our ideas come from and why we have them.
- The seventeenth-century philosopher John Locke argued that ideas are caused by external objects; the Irish philosopher George Berkeley rejected this view and claimed that there are no external objects.
- Hume attempted to offer general principles that explain why some ideas give rise to others.

Core Question

Eighteenth-century philosophers explored the question of how the mind works. David Hume's *An Enquiry Concerning Human Understanding* fits squarely into this tradition.

Hume's contemporaries believed that the contents of the mind are made up of ideas—the mental "objects" that come into being when we have a thought. A principal question they asked was how and why ideas give rise to other ideas. If we understood that, they thought, we would understand the principles that govern the operations of the mind.

Philosophers of this period understood all mental states and operations in terms of ideas. Centrally, this includes sense perceptions and beliefs. But it also includes memories, emotions, pleasure and pain, and all other aspects of our mental lives. In each case, philosophers asked where these ideas came from, and how one idea may cause another to occur.

They also asked a related question: Do our ideas represent the world accurately? In sense experience, for example, do we see the world as it really is? Are our beliefs about the world true?

So the issue was in part a psychological one about how the mind works and in part an epistemological* one, about whether and how we can gain genuine knowledge of the world.

> *"The understanding, like the eye, while it makes us see, and perceive all other things, takes no notice of itself. And it requires art and pains to set it at a distance, and make it its own object."*
> ——Thomas Paine, *Common Sense*, John Locke, *An Essay Concerning Human Understanding*

The Participants

Hume's most important predecessors in the tradition of British empiricism* were John Locke and George Berkeley. Both of these thinkers adopted the view that all our ideas originate in sense experience. Just as one could not think of a color—or imagine it, or remember it—without having first seen the color, they thought the same was true of all our ideas.

Both thinkers went on to ask if our ideas indeed resemble the external world at all. When I see a green patch, for example, does my idea of green correspond to a green patch that really exists in the world? Here, Locke and Berkeley differ.

Locke believed that ideas are caused by an external objects. If you look at a green cup, for example, then the cup is the cause of your idea of green.

Nevertheless, Locke thought, that idea is not *exactly like* the object. For example, the color green you see does not actually exist in the physical world. Your idea of the color depends on different textures in the outside world that reflect light of different wavelengths. So, although the ideas we hold are caused by the external world, they do not always resemble it.

The view that there is an external world for ideas to correspond to is known as "realism."* Berkeley went against realism, instead putting forward an alternative view, often called "idealism."* According to Berkeley, we have no reason to suppose there is any external world corresponding to our ideas. After all, we cannot see such a world directly. When we try to compare our ideas with the world, we can only do so using sense experience, in the process creating further ideas.

The Contemporary Debate

Hume was influenced by both Locke and Berkeley (Locke, to whom he often refers by name, especially). He was not, however, satisfied with Locke's practice of referring to all the objects of thought and perception as "ideas." He thought that doing so overlooked important distinctions.

In particular, Hume distinguished between the objects of sense experience and the objects of thought (including the objects of imagination and memory, and so on). He called the objects of sense experience "impressions," and the others "ideas." Hume expressed the empiricist principle that everything in the mind comes from the senses in this way: all ideas are copies of impressions.[1]

Hume also wanted to explain why certain ideas occur in the mind. Suppose that, whenever I smell coffee, I think of the taste of coffee. One idea (the smell of coffee) has given rise to another (the taste of coffee). Hume wanted to formulate a few general principles that would show why one idea often follows another.

Hume is sometimes thought of as an idealist, like Berkeley. But when it comes to the question of whether our ideas correspond to external objects, Hume is neither an idealist nor a realist: He is simply not interested. Instead, he is interested in the ideas themselves, and in particular in why one idea causes another to occur.

---

1. David Hume, *An Enquiry Concerning Human Understanding* (Cambridge: Cambridge University Press, 2007), 14–15.

MODULE 4
THE AUTHOR'S CONTRIBUTION

KEY POINTS
- Hume argued that many of our beliefs about the world are not based on reason.
- He both explained the workings of human reason and showed its limitations.
- Other philosophers of the time explained the origins of our beliefs—for example, our moral beliefs—by reference to emotion rather than to reason.

Author's Aims

David Hume describes his *An Enquiry Concerning Human Understanding* as dealing with "the science of human nature,"[1] an attempt to explain facts about the human mind. Since he considers human beings as reasoning and believing, he wishes to explain why we think about the world as we do. This project has both positive and negative aspects. On one hand, it involves achieving a new scientific understanding of the mind. But on the other hand the project casts doubt on much of what human beings believe, since it argues that many of our beliefs—such as religious or philosophical beliefs—have no basis in reason. Thus the project encourages a sort of skepticism,* the view that genuine knowledge of the world is impossible.

Enquiry has struck many, from Immanuel Kant* onwards, as an extremely consistent application of empiricist* principles to the study of the mind. Hume follows his argument to its conclusions, even if those conclusions (like that of skepticism) can seem strange and disturbing. Skepticism suggests that our ordinary, everyday beliefs have no grounding in reality, so that a true understanding of the world will forever be beyond our grasp. Some have even taken Hume to have unintentionally undermined empiricism by pushing it to its logical conclusion, showing that if empiricism is true, then skepticism must also be true.

The issue of skepticism can, however, become a barrier to understanding Hume's project. Hume's main aim is not to *change* our beliefs about the world, but rather to *understand* them. His primary interest is psychology—the study of mental processes—not epistemology, the study of knowledge itself. To present Hume primarily as a destructive philosopher who wishes to undermine beliefs that he argues are not grounded in reason distorts his intentions. Indeed, at the end of *Enquiry* Hume suggests that, for the purposes of ordinary life, one can accept his argument without destroying one's world view. Hume accepts that it is natural for human beings to form beliefs that cannot be rationally justified. For example, when I hear birdsong I almost automatically form the belief that there are birds nearby, and no philosophical argument can stop me from forming that belief. That's just part of human nature. Hume does not argue that there is anything wrong with forming beliefs that go beyond the evidence, or that we should cease to do so.

> *"Reason is and ought only to be the slave of the passions, and can never pretend to any other office than to serve and obey them."*
> —— David Hume, *A Treatise of Human Nature*

Approach

David Hume undertook a scientific investigation of human nature, and in particular of the human mind. He wanted to understand how the mind works, and why human beings think as we do. In particular, he aimed to identify the basic principles that govern the operations of the mind. Not content with observing and recording various mental phenomena, he sought to identify the mind's most general features.

In the opening chapter of his *Enquiry*, Hume defended his project, noting that the question is not just interesting, but is *essential* to answer.[2] People need an accurate and well-grounded picture of human nature to achieve their aims and cultivate a good life.

Hume also puts forward a different justification for his interest. It is part of human nature that people will always attempt to understand the world, even if it means asking perplexing and difficult theoretical questions that may well be beyond the capacity of the human mind to answer. Understanding the limits of the human mind would help us to work out which questions our mental abilities are capable of answering, and those that are not. In this way, the success of Hume's project would mean defining the boundaries of the human intellect.

Contribution In Context

Hume regarded his theory of the mind as his life's work. He first proposed this theory in his three-volume work *A Treatise of*

Human Nature, but its reception disappointed him. He intended the *Enquiry* to be a shorter, more accessible introduction to some of his principal ideas.

Hume's approach to psychology had a predecessor in the work of Francis Hutcheson,* a Scottish philosopher who was something of a mentor to Hume. Hutcheson's interests lay particularly in the fields of morality (the principles behind right and wrong) and aesthetics (the principles concerned with nature and beauty). He explained that our judgments about morality and about beauty did not stem from reasoning but from what he called the "sentiments"—what we would call today "emotions." On this point, Hume agreed with Hutcheson. But Hume went further. He argued that reason was less important than was often thought, not only in morals and aesthetics but also in our other beliefs about the world, including those about nature.

Hutcheson exchanged letters with Hume on philosophical matters, and Hume admired him enormously. But the friendship soured when Hutcheson opposed Hume's application for a post at the University of Edinburgh because of Hume's views on religion, an action he found hugely disappointing.[3]

---

1. David Hume, *An Enquiry Concerning Human Understanding* (Cambridge: Cambridge University Press, 2007), 3.
2. Hume, *Enquiry*, 3–13.
3. James Moore, "Hutcheson and Hume," in *Hume and Hume's Connexions*, ed. M. A. Stewart and John P. Wright (Edinburgh: Edinburgh University Press, 1990), 23–57.

SECTION 2
IDEAS

MODULE 5
MAIN IDEAS

KEY POINTS

- Hume makes a distinction between two sorts of questioning: Relations of ideas and matters of fact. Relations of ideas have to do mostly with mathematics; matters of fact concern the external world and our knowledge of them requires observation and experiment.
- Hume argues that our beliefs about causal relations—the idea that one thing leads to another—rest on mental habits rather than on observation.
- The *Enquiry* is a briefer and more accessible introduction to ideas explained in his earlier three-volume *Treatise of Human Nature*.

Key Themes

David Hume, in his *An Enquiry Concerning Human Understanding*, argues that human beings engage in two sorts of inquiry, or questioning: "matters of fact"* and "relations of ideas."*[1]

The second kind of inquiry, about how ideas relate to each other, can only be accomplished by using reason. And Hume believes its only valid use lies in one discipline: mathematics. In his view, everything outside of mathematics must rely on facts gained by conducting research and experiments. Books of metaphysics or theology that do not draw on experimental results can only contain "sophistry* and illusion"—false arguments and imagined truths. He urges us to "commit [such works], then, to the flames."[2]

The first sort of inquiry he defines—for "matters of fact"

about anything in the natural world—requires empirical research and experiments. Unfortunately, Hume notes, humans have a habit of abandoning empirical knowledge and instead basing reasoning about matters of fact on observation. But observation by itself cannot explain why we hold the beliefs we do. We often believe things that mere observation cannot justify, particularly in regard to the external world. Hume traces this to our beliefs about causation.

> "Custom, then, is the great guide of human life. It is that principle alone which renders our experience useful to us, and makes us expect, for the future, a similar train of events with those that have appeared in the past."
>
> —— David Hume, *An Enquiry Concerning Human Understanding*

Exploring The Ideas

When Hume writes that "All reasonings concerning matters of fact seem to be founded on the relation of *Cause and Effect*,"[3] he is arguing that our knowledge of the external world depends on our beliefs about causal relations—how one event will cause another event to occur. When I hear the sound of raindrops on the window and conclude that it is raining, for instance, I am using my knowledge of the fact that rain causes that sound.

But Hume argues that experience is never enough to justify the belief that one event *has* caused another. All we can actually understand is that events succeed each other with a certain regularity and predictability. On the basis of experience alone, we can never reach the conclusion that one event happened *because of* another. Suppose that, watching a game of pool, I see one ball hitting another, causing it to move. Hume thinks that, strictly speaking, all I see when this occurs is that both balls move, not that the first ball caused the movement of the second. In the terms of Hume's empiricism,* we do not have any understanding of causal relations between the two pool balls.

Why then do we hold beliefs about causation? We do so because our minds are governed by what he calls "custom and habit": custom, Hume says, is "the great guide of human life."[4] When we notice a "constant conjunction" between two different events—for example, the first pool ball hitting the second, and the second beginning to move—we automatically expect that the next time we observe pool balls the same thing will occur. Anyone who has tried to learn the game can confirm that this is not always the case.

Having noticed certain patterns (that fire is hot, say, or that snow is cold), we are naturally inclined to expect those patterns to continue to be the same in the future, even though we can never *show* that they will. We expect regularity, not because we have empirical evidence of such regularity, but rather because it is in our nature to expect patterns to repeat. One conclusion Hume draws is that we have no good reason to expect the future to be like the past. Just because we have always found snow to be cold, it does not follow that we will continue to find it cold in the future.

Language And Expression

Although Hume had expressed his main argument in an earlier

work, he later wrote of it that he "had always entertained a notion, that my want of success in publishing the *Treatise of Human Nature*, had proceeded more from the manner than the matter."[5] If he had written the *Treatise* in too obscure a voice, Hume thought that a shorter, easier-to-read version would attract a greater audience. And although he was right, the work did not gain a wide readership until after his death.

A beautifully written book, *Enquiry* has helped win Hume a reputation as one of the best writers of philosophical prose in the English language, if not *the* best. Although its language is by now old-fashioned, it still remains accessible to modern readers, attractively written in relatively simple English.

Enquiry's success may have influenced the way Hume has been interpreted. Readers sometimes think of Hume as mostly interested in epistemological* questions (that is, investigating the origin, nature and limits of human knowledge) and particularly questions about skepticism.* The three-volume *Treatise* makes it clear that this is only part of Hume's concerns. His aim—to formulate a theory of the human mind—is much broader, and skepticism is only one of the issues that arises from that project. In general, Hume's interests are more psychological, as his readers would see if they tackled the more comprehensive *Treatise*.

---

1. David Hume, *An Enquiry Concerning Human Understanding* (Cambridge: Cambridge University Press, 2007), 28.

2. Hume, *Enquiry*, 144.
3. Hume, *Enquiry*, 29.
4. Hume, *Enquiry*, 45.
5. David Hume, "My Own Life," in *The Cambridge Companion to Hume*, ed. David Fate Norton (Cambridge: Cambridge University Press, 1993), 352.

MODULE 6
SECONDARY IDEAS

KEY POINTS

* Hume argued against believing accounts of miracles, and against the view that, since God is good, there is an afterlife that compensates for the evils of this life.
* Hume's arguments concerning religion were very controversial.
* The argument against belief in miracles has been influential both in philosophy of religion and in epistemology.*

Other Ideas

In the later chapters of *An Enquiry Concerning Human Understanding*, David Hume makes skeptical* arguments about religion in general, and in particular about the Christian religion, which was dominant in Europe when the book was published in 1748. While perhaps not the principal point of the book, these arguments have nevertheless proven very influential.

First, Hume tackles the issue of miracles.[1] Christians argued that many miracles had occurred in the early history of the Church, as recorded in lives of the saints and other contemporary sources. The question arises of whether such sources are trustworthy. If they are to be believed, they seem to offer good reason to accept Christianity.

Hume argues, however, that the reports are not trustworthy because they cannot be scientifically verified. As a good empiricist, Hume argues that testimony,* even that of a saint, should be accepted only when it is the same as our own first-hand experience of the world. Further, Hume says, given that Christianity "cannot be believed by any reasonable person"[2] without a miracle, one must doubt the truth of Christianity itself.

Second, Hume addresses the Christian notion of the perfect power and goodness of God.[3] He does not make this argument in his own voice, but, rather, uses the literary device of reporting a conversation he supposedly had with a friend. It may be that Hume was wary of identifying himself with the conclusion of the argument, given its radical and anti-establishment implications. Christians believed that, since God is infinitely good and powerful, we have reason to believe that the imperfections and evils of this world will be compensated for in the afterlife. Hume argues against this idea.

> "We may conclude, that the Christian religion not only was at first attended with miracles, but even at this day cannot be believed by any reasonable person without one. Mere reason is insufficient to convince us of its veracity; and whoever is moved by faith to assent to it, is conscious of a continued miracle in his own person, which subverts all the principles of his understanding, and gives him a determination to believe what is most contrary to custom and experience."
> ——David Hume, *Natural History of Religion*

Exploring The Ideas

In Hume's definition, a miracle is not merely an unusual or surprising event. It is a suspension of the laws of nature, during which regularities in nature that have otherwise always been observed to be true seem to break down. So a miracle, by definition, is an event of a sort that has always been observed not to occur. In this circumstance, Hume argues, it is more reasonable to suppose that testimony of miracles is false (whether because the reporters were innocently mistaken, or distorted the feat through misinterpretation, or purposefully intended to deceive) than to believe that miracles have actually occurred.

"No testimony is sufficient to establish a miracle," Hume writes, "unless the testimony be of such a kind that its falsehood would be more miraculous than the fact which it endeavors to establish."[4]

Following Hume's view that all beliefs should be based on empirical* evidence, we can only believe that God is powerful and good to the extent that the evidence suggests that is true. Christians make a mistake when they suppose that, for example, there must be some reason for evils in the world, whether or not we can discover the reason. Similarly, they are mistaken when they argue that given the imperfect nature of the world, there must be a better afterlife. In holding these beliefs, Hume argues, they assume that God is more perfect than the evidence warrants.

These arguments, highly radical and original in Hume's time, had enormous influence in subsequent efforts to arrive at a rational and evidence-based appraisal of religious belief. In the case of the argument concerning miracles, Hume has been influential in another way, especially in recent times. The argument has become a classic text in debates about the epistemology* of testimony: that is, the use of the word of others, whether spoken or written, as a source of knowledge.⁵

Overlooked

An Enquiry Concerning Human Understanding is a short work that has been intensively studied for over two centuries. Every section of the book has received a great deal of attention. Nevertheless, especially until recently, certain aspects of it have been relatively overlooked. One of these is the depth of Hume's engagement with the ancient Greek tradition of skepticism.* Skepticism had often featured in philosophy as a challenge, with philosophers seeking to refute the skeptic by proving that knowledge is possible. But Hume found another attitude in the Greek tradition: skepticism as a positive vision of how to live.

Hume showed that while many of our beliefs are not based entirely on reason, they are the products of non-rational aspects of human nature: the emotions, for example, and our animal instincts and expectations. He did not see this as a problem to be put right. He recognized that reason alone can never be enough to ground a world view—we could never rebuild our belief system based solely on reason. Instead, Hume felt that we should simply accept the fundamentally non-rational basis of many of our beliefs. This parallels the thinking of the Pyrrhonian skeptics, followers of the ancient Greek philosopher Pyrrho of Elis*. Pyrrhonian skeptics believed that since human beings were not capable of acquiring knowledge, we should suspend judgment about the ways the world is and act according to our natural instincts rather than our beliefs.

Hume differs from the ancient skeptics, however. At the end of *Enquiry* he writes: "The great subverter of Pyrrhonism or the excessive principles of scepticism is action, and employment, and the occupations of common life."[6] He thought that it is part of human nature to believe, and one cannot live life without forming beliefs. Hume recommends leaving skeptical concerns behind in everyday life: not because they have been disproved, but because we must ignore them for practical purposes.

---

1. David Hume, *An Enquiry Concerning Human Understanding* (Cambridge: Cambridge University Press, 2007), 96–116.
2. Hume, *Enquiry*, 116.
3. Hume, *Enquiry*, 117–130.
4. Hume, *Enquiry*, 101.
5. See the essays in *The Epistemology of Testimony*, ed. Jennifer Lackey and Ernest Sosa (Oxford: Oxford University Press, 2006).
6. Hume, *Enquiry*, 139–140.

MODULE 7
ACHIEVEMENT

KEY POINTS

- Hume's skeptical* arguments, especially those about causation and belief in miracles, have been widely studied and accepted.
- Later philosophers often found inspiration for their own projects in Hume's writings.
- Especially since the work of German philosopher Immanuel Kant* in the late eighteenth century, Hume has been read as making a skeptical challenge to knowledge. His larger project, of formulating a theory of the human mind, has sometimes been ignored.

Assessing The Argument

David Hume pursues both philosophy and psychology in *An Enquiry Concerning Human Understanding*. On the one hand, the project is epistemological.* Hume the philosopher assesses certain claims we make about our knowledge (those about causes and effects, or about miracles, for example). He is broadly skeptical of these claims, showing how weak our reasons for making them are.

On the other hand, Hume the scientist puts forward a psychological theory about of the workings of the mind. He is interested in explaining why our minds work as they do, and why we believe what we believe. He is not interested in assessing our beliefs; he wants to explain them.

There is reason to think that formulating a theory of the mind is in fact Hume's main purpose in writing the *Enquiry*. He wrote the book as a brief introduction to the ideas articulated in his *Treatise of Human Nature*, describing it as "an attempt to introduce the experimental method of reasoning into moral subjects." In short, the *Treatise* was an attempt to apply scientific reasoning to the study of human beings.

Hume's arguments about causal belief and belief in miracles have been very influential. Everyone who writes about these topics today must confront his position. Indeed, many have thought that Hume is clearly correct in his arguments on these topics. The twentieth century Australian philosopher J. L. Mackie,* for example, argued this point in his well-known book *The Miracle of Theism*.[1] Paradoxically, the very success and prominence of Hume's arguments has often caused people to lose sight of his overall psychological project. His arguments in psychology may have been more important to him than his arguments in epistemology* (that is, his theory of knowledge). But it is the latter which have had the most lasting influence.

> *"David Hume is one of the most important among philosophers, because he developed to its logical conclusion the empirical philosophy of Locke and Berkeley, and by making it self-consistent made it incredible. He represents, in a certain sense, a dead end: in his direction, it is impossible to go further."*
> —— Bertrand Russell, *History of Western Philosophy*

Achievement In Context

In the nineteenth and early twentieth centuries, many commentators, influenced by the German philosopher Immanuel Kant,* took Hume to be primarily a skeptic who provided a challenge to our established beliefs about the world. The role of the post-Humean philosopher was to find out whether these beliefs could be defended against the criticisms leveled at Hume.

But from the mid-twentieth century on, it became more common to see Hume primarily as a naturalist* philosopher (a philosopher who believes that only natural laws affect the behavior of the universe). The most influential early champion of this view was probably Hume's fellow Scotsman Norman Kemp Smith, the author of *The Philosophy of David Hume*.[2] In it, Kemp Smith argued that Hume intended to investigate the human mind according to the principles of natural science, and so understood human beings as part of the natural world.

If scholars have found it difficult to interpret some of Hume's ideas, a good example might be his ideas about causation. Hume argues that we tend to see events as causing each other because of the structure of our minds, rather than any observable evidence. But this leads us to a contentious question: Is Hume simply describing the processes by which humans form beliefs? Or is he expressing skepticism* about whether causal processes exist at all?

For many years, Hume was seen as challenging philosophers to provide a rational justification for our ordinary beliefs about causation. But more recently an alternative interpretation has become popular through books such as *The Secret Connexion* by the British analytic philosopher Galen Strawson.* According to this interpretation, Hume was not casting doubt on the existence of causation but was investigating a completely separate topic altogether, and his psychological explanations of how our beliefs arise work independently of whether those beliefs are true or false.

Limitations

The interpretation of *Enquiry* has shifted greatly over time and, in some ways, from place to place, too. But interest in the book has not waned; no matter where they live, readers across the centuries have found something in it. Readers often see Hume's work as reflecting their own interests and ideas. The early twentieth century, for example, saw the rise of logical empiricism, or logical positivism,* a movement that shared Hume's belief that the only valid facts were those that could be scientifically verified. For the logical positivists, Hume was a forerunner. Later, naturalist philosophers reinterpeted Hume as believing that philosophy and science are engaged in the same project and use essentially the same methods.

Philosophers in continental Europe have often popularized views different from those of their counterparts in Britain and North America, so it's not surprising that they differ on their interpretation of Hume and his importance to the discipline. The German phenomenologist* Edmund Husserl,* in his book *The Crisis of European Sciences*,[3] interprets Hume as showing the "bankruptcy" of empiricist* philosophy by reducing it to absurdity. Hume's argument shows how empiricism leads to skepticism* and solipsism*—the belief that the only thing one can know for certain is oneself: * If experience is the sole source of knowledge, we cannot be sure that the external world or even other people exist. Husserl believed that Hume's work demonstrated the need for a new start in philosophy that would avoid these absurd results.

In his *Empiricism and Subjectivity*,[4] the French philosopher Gilles Deleuze* claims Hume as a predecessor by interpreting him as an anti-foundationalist (that is, someone who believes that philosophy should not attempt to find anything more certain or basic than our immediate experience of ourselves and of the world). Deleuze admired Hume's denial of metaphysical foundations (what is there and what is it like?) for both the self and for knowledge.

---

1. J. L. Mackie, *The Miracle of Theism: Arguments For and Against the Existence of God* (Oxford: Oxford University Press, 1982).
2. Norman Kemp Smith, *The Philosophy of David Hume* (London: Macmillan, 1941).
3. Edmund Husserl, *The Crisis of the European Sciences and Transcendental Phenomenology*, trans. David Carr (Evanston: Northwestern University Press, 1970).
4. Gilles Deleuze, *Empiricism and Subjectivity*, trans. Constantin V. Boundas (New York: Columbia University Press, 1991).

MODULE 8
PLACE IN THE AUTHOR'S WORK

KEY POINTS
* Hume aimed throughout his life to construct a science of human nature.
* *Enquiry* restates many of the views that Hume had published in his earlier, three-volume *Treatise of Human Nature*.
* Hume's reputation is now based largely on the *Enquiry* and volume one of the *Treatise*.

Positioning

When David Hume published *An Enquiry Concerning Human Understanding* he was 37 years old and had not yet gained any fame as an author. By his own account, his philosophy began to take shape when he was still a teenager, and, in fact, he had put forward many of *Enquiry*'s arguments and theories a decade earlier in *A Treatise of Human Nature*, a work he began writing when he was only 23.

The *Treatise* is a long and difficult work that was not widely read when it was first published. Hume hoped that the shorter and more accessible *Enquiry* would win his ideas a wider audience, which it did—but not until after Hume's death. The only widespread fame Hume won during his lifetime came from his writings on history and his essays for popular audiences, not from his philosophical work.

Hume never changed his mind about the basic nature of his philosophical project, nor about his most important conclusions:

Early and late, he wanted to construct a science of human nature as a systematic explanation of human beings as thinking, feeling and acting creatures. The *Treatise* was an attempt to cover the whole of this vast field. In the shorter *Enquiry*, Hume focused his attention more narrowly on human understanding, and in particular on human beings as believing and knowing subjects. He asks why we believe what we believe.

> "Never literary attempt was more unfortunate than my Treatise of Human Nature. It fell dead-born from the press, without even reaching such distinction, as even to excite a murmur among the zealots."
> —— David Hume, "My Own Life"

Integration

The results Hume reaches in both the *Treatise* and *Enquiry* were important to all his philosophical writings. Reason played a limited role in his explanations of human nature. In Hume's view, much of what we do and think results from our nature, not just as reasoning beings, but as beings with emotions and instincts and expectations that have nothing to do with rationality.

This view leads to skepticism* about certain beliefs, especially those about religion: Hume doubts that we hold the religious beliefs we do because we are persuaded by arguments or evidence. In the absence of such evidence, Hume saw no reason to hold religious beliefs. But that was a very controversial argument in the eighteenth century—indeed, it will still raise hackles in some circles today. So Hume chose to omit many of his religious arguments from the *Treatise*. Later in his life he argued against a belief in God, especially in his last work, *Dialogues Concerning Natural Religion*, a book so controversial that he said it should not be published until after his death.

Another conclusion Hume reaches is the importance of the emotions—or, as Hume called them, the "sentiments"—in our mental lives. This led him to views about morality (the principles behind right and wrong) and aesthetics (the principles concerned with nature and beauty) that he expressed in other writings, including a very popular volume of *Essays*. In the important essay "Of the Standard of Taste," published in 1757, Hume argued that when we make judgments about beauty, we base them on sentiment rather than objective reality. So those judgments reflect nothing more than the nature of the human being who makes them.[1]

Significance

The *Enquiry* is one of Hume's most important and enduringly popular works. Along with Book One of the *Treatise*, with which it has a lot in common, it is the definitive statement of Hume's ideas about human understanding and knowledge. Hume's only comparably important philosophical works are Books Two and Three of the *Treatise*, in which he deals with the emotions and morality respectively.

In other words, Hume's reputation as one of the most important philosophers in the western tradition largely depends on two works: *Enquiry* and the *Treatise*.

Almost every section of *Enquiry* has given rise to philosophical debate. The sections on knowledge and skepticism are considered classics of epistemology.* The section on miracles has been important in the philosophy of religion, just as the discussion of free will has been important in metaphysics.* Perhaps most importantly of all, the section on our knowledge of causal relations has given rise to the problem of induction,* a central problem in the philosophy of science. Induction is the process of finding general principles on the basis of particular observations. It is usually regarded as a crucial element of scientific discovery.

There is also a lively debate on how to interpret Hume correctly. Despite the clarity of his writing style, there is considerable disagreement on the meaning and purpose of his overall project, with philosophers in each period seeming to find their own version of Hume.

---

1. David Hume, *Essays: Moral, Political, and Literary* (Indianapolis: Liberty Classics, 1985).

SECTION 3
IMPACT

MODULE 9
THE FIRST RESPONSES

KEY POINTS

* Critics attacked Hume's theory of ideas and his account of causation.
* Hume countered that his critics believed in "innate ideas." This was tantamount to calling them old-fashioned thinkers.
* Kant and others felt that Hume's philosophy leads to skepticism,* and must be countered if skepticism is to be avoided.

Criticism

Few philosophers read and responded to David Hume's arguments in *An Enquiry Concerning Human Understanding* during his lifetime. The most important thinker to do so was another Scottish philosopher, Thomas Reid,* in his book *Inquiry into the Human Mind on the Principles of Common Sense*, first published in 1764.¹

Reid argued against the basic assumption of Hume's philosophy (what Reid called "the way of ideas"). Other important thinkers of the period, John Locke* and George Berkeley* among them, also shared this assumption. According to Hume and others who supported the way of ideas, we never perceive and think of things in the external world directly; instead, we only form mental entities or ideas of them. For example: when I see an orange ball, my mind forms an idea of a circular orange object. What I see is this idea, not the physical ball. The mind does not touch external objects themselves.

Reid argued that this was a mistake. In his view the mind is not made up of *ideas* (that is, things we see, or think of) but of *activities*, the acts of seeing and thinking. Typically, the objects of our seeing and thinking exist as physical objects outside the mind. So Reid would say that I directly perceive the orange ball; the ball does not reach my mind via an idea or any other intermediary.

Hume argued that human beings base our belief in causal relations merely on observations of regularity in nature; Reid replied that such observations cannot provide the basis of an adequate account of causation. We regularly observe that day follows night, but we do not believe that night causes the day. Further, sometimes we observe a singular example of causation. For instance, if I see a bird fly into and crack a window, I conclude that the bird caused the window to crack, even though I've never seen a bird crack a window before and perhaps never will again. In Reid's view causation cannot be understood in terms of regularly observed patterns in nature.

> "I freely admit the remembrance of David Hume was the very thing that many years ago first interrupted my dogmatic slumber and gave a completely different direction to my researches in the field of speculative philosophy."
> —— Immanuel Kant, *Prolegomena to Any Future Metaphysics*

Responses

Unfortunately for later scholars, Hume did not frequently respond to the few philosophers who criticized his ideas. He dismissed one critic, the poet and philosopher James Beattie,* outright, calling him (in a letter to his publisher) a "bigoted silly fellow."

Hume did respond briefly, in private correspondence, to Reid, whose criticisms did not impress him. He accused Reid of believing in innate* ideas, ideas we are born with. This contrasted starkly with empiricism*—the belief that we derive our ideas from sense experience. The concept of innate ideas had become very unpopular, especially in Britain, so Hume's use of the phrase was the equivalent of calling Reid an old-fashioned thinker. But Hume may have misunderstood Reid's argument. Reid's point, at least in part, is that perception and thought relate to things outside of us. The objects of perception, for example, are not ideas but things in the world, such as orange balls.

Perhaps we can understand Hume's point by thinking again about causation. Reid said that things have causal powers, but he did not claim that we can perceive those causal powers. So how do our minds even grasp the concept of causation? If it does not come from perception, Hume thought, it must be innate.

In the nineteenth and early twentieth centuries, philosophers generally felt that Hume had won the argument. But during the twentieth century, Reid came to be re-evaluated. Many philosophers today are sympathetic both with direct perception and the idea that causal powers are real. Today, it seems fair to say that some philosophers agree with Hume and others with Reid. After hundreds of years of debate, there has been no agreement on a single position.

Conflict And Consensus

The German philosopher Immanuel Kant,* another of Hume's contemporaries, claimed that when he read Hume's work, he was "awoken from his dogmatic slumber."² Kant found something profoundly disturbing in Hume's argument: He disagreed with it, but he recognized its power and felt it urgently required a response. Kant's later philosophy can be seen, to a large extent, as a response to Hume. For Kant, Hume had shown that we do not derive our knowledge of cause and effect from experience. Nevertheless, science shows that we do have such knowledge. So, Kant argued, our knowledge of cause and effect must be based not on experience but purely on reason. It would have been interesting to see how Hume reacted to this argument, but he died before Kant finally published his response, *Critique of Pure Reason*, in 1781.³

According to Kant, Hume's work highlighted a problem with the scientific method. Science tests very general conclusions by looking at particular instances. For example, we claim that all animals with hearts also have kidneys, and we test this hypothesis by checking every species that we can. But such testing can never be enough to establish the general conclusion, because we might discover a new species that has a heart but not a kidney—a complication called the problem of induction.* Hume was thought to have shown that inductive reasoning was inadequate to establish scientific conclusions. As a result, philosophers thought that to respond to Hume's arguments they had either to show that scientific method was not open to the problem of induction, or to accept that scientific knowledge is impossible.

---

1. Thomas Reid, *An Inquiry into the Human Mind on the Principles of Common Sense* (University Park: Pennsylvania State University Press, 1997).
2. Immanuel Kant, *Prolegomena to Any Future Metaphysics*, trans. and ed. Gary Hatfield (Cambridge: Cambridge University Press, 1997), 10.
3. Immanuel Kant, *Critique of Pure Reason*, translated by Paul Guyer and Allen W. Wood (Cambridge: Cambridge University Press, 1997).

MODULE 10
THE EVOLVING DEBATE

KEY POINTS

- Hume's *Enquiry* spurred an enduring debate about the possibility of empirical knowledge and the validity of induction*, that is, testing general conclusions by looking at particular instances.
- Its arguments influenced philosophers such as the logical positivists to dismiss metaphysics* as meaningless.
- Contemporary philosophical naturalists* have learned much from Hume.

Uses And Problems

Philosophers in the nineteenth and twentieth centuries reading *An Enquiry Concerning Human Understanding* and David Hume's other works believed that he had demonstrated the limits of empiricism.* Hume assumed that empiricism is true: all our beliefs about the world are based on sensory experience alone. But he also showed how little could ultimately be proven by sensory experience. If empiricism is "correct," and we reason entirely empirically, we cannot reach any general truths about the world, or gain insight into the causal order of nature, let alone reach beyond the natural world to discover metaphysical truths about God or immortality. Hume's work also made the problem of induction a major challenge for epistemology*—the philosophical study of knowledge—and the philosophy of science.

Some theorists, among them, the nineteenth-century British

philosopher and economist John Stuart Mill,* responded to Hume by outlining a scientific method which, they thought, would generate rationally believable but not entirely certain results if followed well.[1]

The method of induction they advocated would be rational—distinguishing between good and bad science—but it would also necessarily be untrustworthy. One could never be certain that the good science is true. In the twentieth century, the philosopher Karl Popper* made a more radical proposal: that science does not need to use induction at all.[2] Popper noted that the general theories scientists put forward are merely guesses and are not based on evidence; scientific rigor comes into play only by devising experiments to test these guesses. In Popper's view, science consists only in *disproving* hypotheses (or assumptions) through experiment, not in *establishing* them.

Another tradition, one that began with the work of the German philosopher Immanuel Kant,* proposed a different response to Hume's ideas. Kant and his followers agreed that sensory experience alone could not establish knowledge about the world. Accordingly, they thought, we need certain *a priori** principles— that is, principles known independently of experience. Knowledge that the world is governed by causation, Kant thought, for example, is *a priori*.

But how can such *a priori* principles be justified? How can they be distinguished from irrational beliefs or mere prejudices? Although at this point questions become very complicated, Kant thought (in brief) that *a priori* principles could only be justified insofar as they applied to the realm of possible experience. We can be sure that everything we are capable of experiencing is governed by causation, but we cannot be sure that everything that exists is so governed.

> "When we run over libraries, persuaded of these principles, what havoc must we make? If we take in our hand any volume; of divinity or school metaphysics, for instance; let us ask, Does it contain any abstract reasoning concerning quantity or number? No. Does it contain any experimental reasoning concerning matter of fact and existence? No. Commit it then to the flames: For it can contain nothing but sophistry and illusion."
>
> —— David Hume, *An Enquiry Concerning Human Understanding*

Schools Of Thought

Kant's theory relates to another major evolutionary effect of Hume's thought. Hume taught many philosophers to be suspicious of metaphysics,* traditionally understood as the study of the fundamental nature of reality. But Hume emphasizes the ways in which our knowledge of the world is limited by the sort of creatures we are. His work made many thinkers doubt that human beings were capable of acquiring metaphysical knowledge. Anti-metaphysical thinkers of the twentieth century, notably logical-positivist philosophers such as Rudolf Carnap,* a leading philosopher in Vienna before World War II,* and his British contemporary A. J. Ayer,* were greatly influenced by Hume, either directly or through Kant.³

Indeed, logical-positivist philosophy can be seen as a radicalization of Hume's. Hume argues that only two things can improve our knowledge and understanding of the world: first, the kinds of empiricism found in the sciences, where observations and experiments are relied on; and second, mathematics. In Hume's view, disciplines such as metaphysics and theology,* which belong to neither category, do not add to knowledge. The logical positivists took this line of reasoning even further, saying that these other disciplines are not meaningful at all. As the logical positivists see it, metaphysicians and theologians not only fail to discover new truths about the world, they actually talk nonsense. Statements like "God made the world," if they cannot be tested by experiment and observations, have no meaning at all.

In Current Scholarship

Today's political scholars recognize Paine's *Common Sense* as a Hume's influence survived the decline of logical positivism's popularity in the middle of the twentieth century, a time when it became more common to interpret him as a philosophical naturalist.* Naturalists see philosophers and scientists as engaged in the same project of understanding the natural world. Naturalists have found inspiration in Hume's works, seeing their primary purpose as to create a science of the mind, and in this way to bring human beings more fully into the domain of science.

This project made sense to naturalistic philosophers such

as the American academic W. V. Quine,* who argues in his article "Epistemology Naturalized"[4] that epistemology*—the philosophical study of knowledge—should be reconceived as part of psychology. Philosophers interested in knowledge should use scientific methods to study the ways in which knowledge is produced by human beings. This would involve studying the actual operations of the mind (how our perceptions give rise to beliefs, for example). Quine's naturalized epistemology is, as he acknowledges, very much in the spirit of Hume, and more recent philosophers such as Alvin Goldman* have advanced the theory.

More broadly, recent philosophy has moved toward seeing the human mind as part of nature, subject to the same laws as other natural objects and capable of being explained in the same way. This attitude is fundamentally Humean.

---

1. John Stuart Mill, *A System of Logic* (London: John W. Parker, 1843).
2. Karl Popper, *Conjectures and Refutations* (London: Routledge, 2002), 60.
3. A. J. Ayer, *Language, Truth and Logic* (London: Gollancz, 1946); Ayer ed., *Logical Positivism* (New York: Free Press, 1959).
4. W. V. Quine, "Epistemology Naturalized" in *Ontological Relativity and Other Essays* (New York: Columbia, 1969).

MODULE 11
IMPACT AND INFLUENCE TODAY

KEY POINTS

* *Enquiry* is a classic exploration of the limits of empirical* knowledge.
* It challenges the ideas that experience can provide an adequate account of knowledge, and that we can have any real knowledge of necessary truths, except for those which are very trivial.
* Philosophers have responded by attempting to close Hume's gap between experience and theory.

Position

Many of the challenges to contemporary thought presented by David Hume's work, those of *An Enquiry Concerning Human Understanding* especially, come from his strict empiricism.* Empiricism claims that all our knowledge comes from experience. If, therefore, we have beliefs that go beyond what experience can teach us, we can only guess at them; these are things we cannot *know*. Empiricism can lead to certain sorts of skepticism* (that is, the denial that we can attain various forms of knowledge). While many philosophers have agreed with empiricism, few have applied it as consistently as Hume did.

If *Enquiry* has become a philosophical classic, it is partly because it is regarded as presenting a challenge that has yet to be answered. It challenges the idea that experience, as defined in the empiricist tradition, can provide an adequate foundation for our beliefs about the world. Philosophers respond to the challenge in different ways. Some, among them the twentieth century American philosopher W. V. Quine,* accept Hume's argument, and reject the project of providing foundations for knowledge. Others, such as the South African philosopher John McDowell,* regard Hume as demonstrating that the empiricist conception of experience is inadequate. In their view, perceptual experience is richer than Hume thought. With a suitably wide conception of experience, they believe that experience can indeed provide a foundation for knowledge.

> *"I do not see that we are farther along today than where Hume left us. The Humean predicament is the human predicament"*
>
> —— W. V. Quine, "Epistemology Naturalized"

Interaction

Humeans tend towards skepticism* on the issue of causation. Most of us naturally think of events *causing* each other, or of things having causal power. We see a ball hit a window and we see the window smash, so we think that the impact of the ball caused the smashing of the window. Humean skepticism doubts that we are entitled to this belief: all we have experienced is one event following another. We cannot attribute any causation to nature.

Humeans also argue that we cannot know any necessary truths (except perhaps very trivial ones). Hume distinguished between what he called "matters of fact"* and "relations of ideas."* In his view, all truths about the empirical world, the world of nature, are matters of fact. Relations of ideas pertain, rather, to our own concepts.

Mathematics offers relations of ideas: two plus two must always equal four; no other answer is possible. A non-mathematical example of a relation of ideas is the connection between being a bachelor and being unmarried. It is a necessary truth that all bachelors are unmarried; a married man would simply not count as being a bachelor. But Hume argues that such truths only tell us about the content of the concept "bachelor" and not about the real world.

This presents a challenge to philosophers who see themselves as investigating necessary truths about the world—the traditional concept behind metaphysics.* The special sciences, like physics or biology, discover truths about the world that are subject to chance; very general, necessary truths, on the other hand, are the realm of metaphysics.* Humeans doubt there are any such truths for metaphysics to study, or believe that if such truths do exist, we cannot gain any concrete knowledge of them.

The Continuing Debate

Hume denied that perceptual experience on its own is sufficient to yield knowledge about the world. Influenced by the German philosopher Immanuel Kant,* some thinkers respond that perception is richer and is capable of yielding more knowledge than Hume argued. A prominent contemporary promoter of this view is John McDowell, who argues in his book *Mind and World*[1] that perceptual experience is rich in concepts. In his view, the kind of perceptual experience human beings are capable of having depends on our conceptual abilities. Different people see dogs differently, for example, because of the background knowledge we possess about dogs.

Hume makes an important assumption that *empirical* truths—truths that can be discovered by observation and experiment—cannot be *necessary* truths,* because necessary truths are the kinds of things one cannot logically deny. Mathematical truths, for example, seem to be necessary: It is not only true that two plus two is four, but it could not be otherwise. Hume thought that mathematical truths can be arrived at *a priori*,* by using reason on its own, without reference to experience. The truths that we discover empirically can only be contingent truths*; our beliefs about necessity in nature—for example, causal necessity—cannot be established as true by empirical research alone.

In one of the most important philosophical works of recent decades, *Naming and Necessity*,[2] the American analytical philosopher Saul Kripke* argued against this Humean thesis. According to Kripke, some necessary truths can also be empirical; scientists have established this fact. For example, Kripke argues, it is a necessary truth that water is composed of hydrogen and oxygen—any substance that did not have this composition would not be water. But chemists had to do a great deal of empirical research to discover this truth. Kripke has played an important role in restoring metaphysics to a central place in philosophy.

In different ways, both McDowell and Kripke aim to close the Humean gap between experience and theory, helping to vindicate the idea that our beliefs—including our beliefs about causal processes and necessary truths—can sometimes be supported by experience.

---

1. John McDowell, *Mind and World* (Cambridge, Mass.: Harvard University Press, 1996).
2. Saul Kripke, *Naming and Necessity* (Oxford: Blackwell, 1980).

MODULE 12
WHERE NEXT?

KEY POINTS

* The topics discussed in *Enquiry*, including the nature of causation and the nature of mind, remain controversial in philosophy and psychology.
* Some important contemporary thinkers continue to advance Humean solutions to these problems.
* *Enquiry* is a crucial text in the history of empiricism,* naturalism,* and skepticism.*

Potential

Over two hundred years after its publication, philosophers and psychologists still debate many of the arguments David Hume raises in *An Enquiry Concerning Human Understanding*. One such argument revolves around the nature of causation: Are causal laws simply patterns or regularities in nature? Or are causes, rather, real powers that explain why such patterns hold? Take, for example, the claim that smoking causes cancer. Does this mean merely that those who smoke are in fact more likely to contract cancer? Or does it mean there is something in the nature of smoking that brings about cancer?

A second subject for debate is the nature of the mind. Like other empiricists,* Hume believed that everything in the mind comes from experience. Much current discussion revolves around the issue of concepts (that is, the general categories in terms of which we understand the world). For example, when I sort the cutlery into knives, forks and spoons, I am employing three concepts to categorize the contents of the cutlery drawer. The question then arises: Where do my concepts come from? Do they all come from experience? Or are some or all of them derived from some other source such as my genetic inheritance, for example?

> "[Hume's] commanding presence in philosophy lies in the clarity of vision, the fact that time and time again he sees so exactly how things stand with us."
> —— Simon Blackburn*, *How to Read Hume*

Future Directions

Many contemporary philosophers follow or echo various doctrines put forward by Hume. A smaller but still substantial number of philosophers have done work that has been so shaped by Hume that they might be called "Humeans."

One such thinker is the British philosopher Helen Beebee,* a scholar of Hume whose original philosophical work, especially in the field of metaphysics,* also shows his influence. Beebee defends a Humean conception of the laws of nature, those very general laws of the universe which are discovered by science. According to her, these laws do not govern nature. They do not determine what will happen in the universe but, rather, merely describe very general natural patterns.[1] More broadly, Beebee argues that there is no necessity in nature: Everything in nature, including all that can be observed and investigated by natural science, is merely chance.

If Beebee defends a Humean metaphysics, the American philosopher Jesse Prinz* has argued for a Humean philosophy of mind. In his book *Furnishing the Mind*,[2] Prinz argues that we derive concepts from perceptual experience. This is empiricism,* a doctrine that has been frequently criticized since Hume's time. But Prinz offers a sophisticated defense of empiricism, drawing on modern psychology and cognitive science (the study of the mind and its processes). Hume's eighteenth-century world view is, Prinz thinks, largely supported by twenty-first-century science.

Summary

Without a doubt, David Hume's *An Enquiry Concerning Human Understanding* has earned its place as one of the great works of the western philosophical tradition. Despite being a short work, it has profoundly influenced philosophical discussion on a number of different topics and has given rise to several different streams of thought.

Some of the book's influence stems from the consistency and single-mindedness with which Hume pursues the consequences of empiricism.* Like other empiricists, he assumes that everything in the mind comes from the senses. But Hume drew consequences from this assumption that no previous empiricist had drawn. His *Enquiry* put the issue of causation, for example, at the center of philosophical discussion by raising profound doubts about whether causal powers in nature are open to observation. All we can observe, Hume said, are regular, repeated patterns in nature.

Ever since Hume, philosophers have wondered what causation is, and whether there is anything to the notion other than regularity in nature. Hume also cast profound doubts on conventional religious beliefs by questioning whether a belief in miracles could be justified on empiricist grounds.

If *Enquiry* is a pinnacle of the empiricist tradition, it is also a pioneering work in another philosophical tradition: naturalism.* Hume undertook a scientific investigation of the human mind, applying to it the same principles that we use in the study of other parts of nature. Such an approach, if successful, would confirm the status of human beings as simply a part of the natural world, no different to non-human animals; humans have their own distinctive features, but they are not essentially distinct from the rest of nature. Naturalistic philosophers made great advances during the twentieth century and although much of contemporary naturalism would be unrecognizable to Hume, it is still very much in his spirit.

Enquiry is also a landmark in the modern discussion of skepticism,* a challenging epistemological issue* with which philosophers have struggled since the seventeenth century, when René Descartes wrote his major works. Descartes debated with an imaginary skeptical opponent to show that it is, after all, possible to gain genuine knowledge of the world.

Although philosophers differ in their opinions of how successfully Descartes disproved the skeptical argument, Hume's discussion, raising the possibility that skepticism cannot be answered at an intellectual level, was different: how should we live, he asked, given that we cannot disprove the skeptic?

---

1. Helen Beebee, "The Non-Governing Conception of Laws of Nature," *Philosophy and Phenomenological Research* 56 (2000): 571–594.
2. Jesse Prinz, *Furnishing the Mind: Concepts and their Perceptual Basis* (Cambridge: MIT Press, 2002).

GLOSSARY OF TERMS

1. **a priori:** *a priori* knowledge is knowledge held independently of experience.
2. **Church of Scotland:** the Protestant national church of Scotland.
3. **Contingent truths:** things that are true but are not required to be true. A "contingent truth" is the opposite of a "necessary truth". It is true that Berlin is the capital of Germany, for example—but is not a necessary truth, as the capital could just as easily be Bonn.
4. **Empiricism:** the view that all human knowledge comes from experience.
5. **Epistemology:** the philosophical study of knowledge.
6. **Idealism:** the view that there is no reality independent of our minds.
7. **Ideas:** in Hume's theory of the mind, ideas are copies of sense experience, held in the mind. We copy our idea of yellow, for example, from our visual experiences of yellow things.
8. **Impressions:** in Hume's theory of the mind, impressions are sense experiences. The other contents of the mind, ideas, are copies of impressions.
9. **Induction:** the process of assuming general principles from particular instances.
10. **Innateness:** innate characteristics are those with which human beings are born, as opposed to learned characteristics.
11. **Logical positivism:** a radical philosophical movement emphasizing the logical analysis of language. Logical positivists were active from the late 1920s, especially in Austria and Germany.
12. **Matters of fact:** matters concerning the way the world is. For Hume, these can only be known as a result of observation and experiment.
13. **Metaphysics:** an area of *philosophy* that looks to explain the nature of *being* and the *world* around it.
14. **Miracle:** a remarkable event attributed to divine or supernatural causes.
15. **Naturalism:** in philosophy, naturalism is the view that philosophy and science are engaged in the same project and use essentially the same methods.

16. **Necessary truths:** truths that, unlike contingent truths, could not have been otherwise. It is a necessary truth that bachelors are unmarried: no bachelor could possibly be married.

17. **Phenomenology:** the study of the ways in which the world appears to people.

18. **Realism:** the view that the world is independent of the mind.

19. **Relations of ideas:** for Hume, relations of ideas can, unlike matters of fact, be known with certainty independently of experience. They include the truths of mathematics.

20. **Skepticism:** the view that genuine knowledge of the world is impossible.

21. **Scottish Enlightenment:** the name given by historians to a fertile period of development in Scottish science, philosophy and literature during the eighteenth century.

22. **Solipsism:** the view that other people do not exist. Each solipsist believes that he or she is the only existing person.

23. **Sophistry:** the art of producing arguments that are superficially believable but not rationally convincing.

24. **Testimony:** the transmission of knowledge from one person to another, either through speech or through writing.

25. **Theology:** the study of God and religious belief.

26. **World War II (1939–45):** a global war between the vast majority of states, including all the great powers of the time.

PEOPLE MENTIONED IN THE TEXT

1. **A. J. Ayer (1910–89)** was an English philosopher best known for popularizing logical positivism in Britain and the United States.

2. **Pierre Bayle (1647–1706)** was a French philosopher and essayist, who emphasized the limitations of human reason and the impossibility of gaining certain knowledge.

3. **James Beattie (1735–1803)** was a Scottish poet and philosopher best known for his work in moral philosophy.

4. **Helen Beebee** is a British philosopher best known for her work on metaphysics and on Hume.

5. **George Berkeley (1685–1753)** was an Irish philosopher who argued for empiricism and idealism.

6. **Simon Blackburn (b. 1944)** is an English philosopher known for his attempts to popularize the discipline.

7. **Robert Boyle (1627–91)** was an Irish scientist, a founder of chemistry, and one of the most important scientists of his century.

8. **Rudolf Carnap (1891–1970)** was a German philosopher and leader of the logical-positivist movement. He contributed to logic, the philosophy of language and the philosophy of science.

9. **Samuel Clarke (1675–1729)** was an English philosopher and theologian who defended Isaac Newton's philosophical views and argued for the existence of God.

10. **Gilles Deleuze (1925–95)** was a French philosopher best known for his work in metaphysics and the philosophy of art.

11. **René Descartes (1596–1650)** was a French scientist, mathematician and philosopher who is regarded as one of the most important philosophers of the modern era.

12. **Alvin Goldman (b. 1938)** is an American philosopher best known for his work in epistemology.

13. **Edmund Husserl (1859–1938)** was a German philosopher considered to be

the founder of phenomenology (the study of the structures of experience and consciousness).

14. **Francis Hutcheson (1694–1746)** was a Scottish philosopher best known for his moral philosophy and for his theory of the emotions.

15. **James Hutton (1726–97)** was a Scottish scientist who is regarded as the founder of modern geology.

16. **Immanuel Kant (1724–1804)** was a German philosopher who wrote *The Critique of Pure Reason* (1781). He is regarded as perhaps the most influential philosopher of the modern era.

17. **Saul Kripke (b. 1940)** is an American philosopher who has contributed to logic, philosophy of language, and numerous other fields and is widely regarded as one of the most important contemporary philosophers.

18. **John Locke (1632–1704)** was an English philosopher noted for his contributions to epistemology, philosophy of mind and political philosophy.

19. **J. L. Mackie (1917–1981)** was an Australian philosopher who contributed to ethics, metaphysics, and the philosophy of religion.

20. **John McDowell (b. 1942)** is a British philosopher who has written on topics as diverse as Aristotle, ethics, epistemology, and the philosophy of mind.

21. **John Stuart Mill (1806–73)** was an English philosopher, known for his contributions to philosophy of science and to ethics and political philosophy.

22. **Isaac Newton (1642–1727)** was an English scientist, mathematician and philosopher. He is frequently regarded as one of the greatest physicists and mathematicians who ever lived.

23. **Karl Popper (1902–94)** was an Austrian philosopher. He is perhaps one of the best-known philosophers of science of the twentieth century.

24. **Jesse Prinz** is an American philosopher and cognitive scientist who has written both for academic and popular audiences on psychology, the emotions and aesthetics.

25. **Pyrrho of Elis (c. 360–270 B.C.E.)** was an ancient Greek philosopher.

Although he did not write anything, he is thought to have been a radical skeptic who believed that knowledge is impossible and that human beings should not attempt to know anything about the world.

26. **W. V. Quine (1908–2000)** was an American philosopher who contributed to logic, philosophy of language, epistemology, and the philosophy of science.
27. **Thomas Reid (1710–69)** was a Scottish philosopher who is best known today for his theory of perception.
28. **Sextus Empiricus (c. 160–210)** was a Greek physician best known for his writings on epistemology, in which he showed he was in favor of a form of skepticism.
29. **Adam Smith (1723–90)** was a Scottish philosopher and economist, regarded as one of the founders of modern economics.
30. **James St Clair (1688–1762)** was a Scottish soldier and politician.
31. **Galen Strawson (b. 1952)** is a British philosopher who has written on metaphysics, the philosophy of mind, and the history of philosophy.
32. **James Watt (1736–1819)** was a Scottish engineer who invented the modern steam engine.

WORKS CITED

1. Ayer, A. J. *Language, Truth and Logic*. London: Gollancz, 1946.
2. ed., *Logical Positivism*. New York: Free Press, 1959.
3. Beebee, Helen. "The Non-Governing Conception of Laws of Nature." *Philosophy and Phenomenological Research* 56 (2000): 571–594.
4. Deleuze, Gilles. *Empiricism and Subjectivity*. Translated by Constantin V.
5. Boundas. New York: Columbia University Press, 1991.
6. Hume, David. *A Treatise of Human Nature*. Oxford: Oxford University Press, 1978.
7. *Essays Moral, Political and Literary*. Indianopolis: Liberty Classics, 1985.
8. "My Own Life." In *The Cambridge Companion to Hume*. Edited by David Fate Norton. Cambridge: Cambridge University Press, 1993.
9. *An Enquiry Concerning Human Understanding*. Cambridge: Cambridge University Press, 2007.
10. *Dialogues Concerning Natural Religion*. Cambridge: Cambridge University Press, 2007.
11. Husserl, Edmund. *The Crisis of the European Sciences and Transcendental Phenomenology*. Translated by David Carr. Evanston: Northwestern University Press.
12. Kant, Immanuel. *Critique of Pure Reason*. Translated by Paul Guyer and Allen W. Wood. Cambridge: Cambridge University Press, 1997.
13. *Prolegomena to Any Future Metaphysics*. Translated and edited by Gary Hatfield. Cambridge: Cambridge University Press, 1997.
14. Kripke, Saul. *Naming and Necessity*. Oxford: Blackwell, 1980.
15. Lackey, Jennifer and Ernest Sosa, eds. *The Epistemology of Testimony*. Oxford: Oxford University Press, 2006.
16. Mackie, J. L. *The Miracle of Theism: Arguments For and Against the Existence of God*. Oxford: Oxford University Press, 1982.
17. McDowell, John. *Mind and World*. Cambridge, Mass.: Harvard University Press, 1996.
18. Mill, John Stuart. *A System of Logic*. London: John W. Parker, 1843.
19. Moore, James. "Hutcheson and Hume." In *Hume and Hume's Connexions*.

Edited by M. A. Stewart and John P. Wright. Edinburgh: Edinburgh University Press, 1990.

20. Popper, Karl. *Conjectures and Refutations*. London: Routledge, 2002.
21. Prinz, Jesse. *Furnishing the Mind: Concepts and their Perceptual Basis*. Cambridge: MIT Press, 2002.
22. Quine, W.V. "Epistemology Naturalized." In *Ontological Relativity and Other Essays*. New York: Columbia University Press, 1969.
23. Reid, Thomas. *An Enquiry into the Human Mind on the Principles of Common Sense*. University Park, PA: Pennsylvania State University Press, 1997.
24. Smith, Norman Kemp. *The Philosophy of David Hume*. London: Macmillan, 1941.
25. Strawson, Galen. *The Secret Connexion: Causation, Realism and David Hume*. Oxford: Clarendon Press, 1989.
26. Weis, Charles and Frederick Pottle. *Boswell in Extremes, 1776–1778*. New York: McGraw-Hill, 1970.

原书作者简介

大卫·休谟 1711 年出生于苏格兰爱丁堡，他天赋异禀，12 岁就进入爱丁堡大学读书，似乎注定要从事学术事业，然而他的宗教观点却将他推向知识主流之外。他对基督教持怀疑态度，可以说，他不相信上帝。于是休谟成为外交家和作家，被誉为他那个年代中杰出的思想家之一。这种名望一直持续到今天，很多人认为休谟是在以英语写作的哲学家中最伟大的一位。

本书作者简介

迈克·奥沙利文博士是伦敦国王学院哲学系导师，系《维特根斯坦与感知》一书的编者。

世界名著中的批判性思维

《世界思想宝库钥匙丛书》致力于深入浅出地阐释全世界著名思想家的观点，不论是谁、在何处都能了解到，从而推进批判性思维发展。

《世界思想宝库钥匙丛书》与世界顶尖大学的一流学者合作，为一系列学科中最有影响的著作推出新的分析文本，介绍其观点和影响。在这一不断扩展的系列中，每种选入的著作都代表了历经时间考验的思想典范。通过为这些著作提供必要背景、揭示原作者的学术渊源以及说明这些著作所产生的影响，本系列图书希望让读者以新视角看待这些划时代的经典之作。读者应学会思考、运用并挑战这些著作中的观点，而不是简单接受它们。

ABOUT THE AUTHOR OF THE ORIGINAL WORK

Born in Edinburgh, Scotland in 1711, the brilliant **David Hume** entered the University of Edinburgh at the age of 12, seemingly destined for a career in academia. But his religious views put him outside the intellectual mainstream. He was skeptical of Christianity and arguably did not believe in God. So Hume became a diplomat and writer, establishing a reputation as one of the finest thinkers of his generation. That reputation has endured: many believe Hume was the greatest philosopher ever to write in English.

ABOUT THE AUTHORS OF THE ANALYSIS

Dr Michael O'Sullivan is a tutor in the Department of Philosophy, King's College London. He is the editor of *Wittgenstein and Perception*.

ABOUT MACAT
GREAT WORKS FOR CRITICAL THINKING

Macat is focused on making the ideas of the world's great thinkers accessible and comprehensible to everybody, everywhere, in ways that promote the development of enhanced critical thinking skills.

It works with leading academics from the world's top universities to produce new analyses that focus on the ideas and the impact of the most influential works ever written across a wide variety of academic disciplines. Each of the works that sit at the heart of its growing library is an enduring example of great thinking. But by setting them in context—and looking at the influences that shaped their authors, as well as the responses they provoked—Macat encourages readers to look at these classics and game-changers with fresh eyes. Readers learn to think, engage and challenge their ideas, rather than simply accepting them.

批判性思维及《人类理解研究》

首要的批判性思维技巧：分析
次要的批判性思维技巧：推理

大卫·休谟在 1748 年出版的《人类理解研究》是一部帮助重建认识论，也就是知识哲学的现代哲学经典。此书也是一部关于批判性思维技巧分析及推理的经典之作。

分析是理解论争是如何展开并相互适应的。具备较强的分析技巧就能帮助打破论争，顺藤摸瓜找出其依赖的论据，进而理解论争得以推进的各种隐含假设和推理。同时，推理也意味着建立和呈现论争，从而形成对某一特定观点的完整有据、条理清晰的案例。休谟将他的分析技巧应用于人类是如何认识和了解这个世界以及我们的思维是如何工作的这些论争中。从根本上说，他一直试图对人类推理本身进行研究，旨在展现人类思维过程及其局限性，并对人类信念的起源进行探究。

休谟运用他的推理技巧，开创了有关人类知识本质这一问题的持久论争，其结果就是哲学史上最卓越闻名的著作之一——《人类理解研究》。

CRITICAL THINKING AND *AN ENQUIRY CONCERNING HUMAN UNDERSTANDING*

- Primary critical thinking skill: ANALYSIS
- Secondary critical thinking skill: REASONING

David Hume's 1748 *Enquiry Concerning Human Understanding* is a modern philosophical classic that helped reshape epistemology — the philosophy of knowledge. It is also a classic of the critical thinking skills of analysis and reasoning.

Analysis is all about understanding how arguments work and fit together. Having strong analytical skills helps to break down arguments, pull out the evidence on which they rely, and understand the kinds of implicit assumptions and reasons on which they work. Reasoning, meanwhile, means building and presenting arguments, forming well-structured, evidenced, and organised cases for a particular point of view. Hume applied his analytical skills to arguments about how humans know and understand the world, and how our minds work. At base, he was trying to analyse human reason itself — to show the workings and limitations of the human mind, and show the origins of our beliefs.

Hume went on to apply his reasoning skills, creating an enduring argument about the nature of human knowledge. The result was one of the most striking and famous works in the history of philosophy.

《世界思想宝库钥匙丛书》简介

《世界思想宝库钥匙丛书》致力于为一系列在各领域产生重大影响的人文社科类经典著作提供独特的学术探讨。每一本读物都不仅仅是原经典著作的内容摘要，而是介绍并深入研究原经典著作的学术渊源、主要观点和历史影响。这一丛书的目的是提供一套学习资料，以促进读者掌握批判性思维，从而更全面、深刻地去理解重要思想。

每一本读物分为3个部分：学术渊源、学术思想和学术影响，每个部分下有4个小节。这些章节旨在从各个方面研究原经典著作及其反响。

由于独特的体例，每一本读物不但易于阅读，而且另有一项优点：所有读物的编排体例相同，读者在进行某个知识层面的调查或研究时可交叉参阅多本该丛书中的相关读物，从而开启跨领域研究的路径。

为了方便阅读，每本读物最后还列出了术语表和人名表（在书中则以星号*标记），此外还有参考文献。

《世界思想宝库钥匙丛书》与剑桥大学合作，理清了批判性思维的要点，即如何通过6种技能来进行有效思考。其中3种技能让我们能够理解问题，另3种技能让我们有能力解决问题。这6种技能合称为"批判性思维PACIER模式"，它们是：

分析：了解如何建立一个观点；
评估：研究一个观点的优点和缺点；
阐释：对意义所产生的问题加以理解；
创造性思维：提出新的见解，发现新的联系；
解决问题：提出切实有效的解决办法；
理性化思维：创建有说服力的观点。

THE MACAT LIBRARY

The Macat Library is a series of unique academic explorations of seminal works in the humanities and social sciences — books and papers that have had a significant and widely recognised impact on their disciplines. It has been created to serve as much more than just a summary of what lies between the covers of a great book. It illuminates and explores the influences on, ideas of, and impact of that book. Our goal is to offer a learning resource that encourages critical thinking and fosters a better, deeper understanding of important ideas.

Each publication is divided into three Sections: Influences, Ideas, and Impact. Each Section has four Modules. These explore every important facet of the work, and the responses to it.

This Section-Module structure makes a Macat Library book easy to use, but it has another important feature. Because each Macat book is written to the same format, it is possible (and encouraged!) to cross-reference multiple Macat books along the same lines of inquiry or research. This allows the reader to open up interesting interdisciplinary pathways.

To further aid your reading, lists of glossary terms and people mentioned are included at the end of this book (these are indicated by an asterisk [*] throughout) — as well as a list of works cited.

Macat has worked with the University of Cambridge to identify the elements of critical thinking and understand the ways in which six different skills combine to enable effective thinking.

Three allow us to fully understand a problem; three more give us the tools to solve it. Together, these six skills make up the PACIER model of critical thinking. They are:

ANALYSIS — understanding how an argument is built
EVALUATION — exploring the strengths and weaknesses of an argument
INTERPRETATION — understanding issues of meaning
CREATIVE THINKING — coming up with new ideas and fresh connections
PROBLEM-SOLVING — producing strong solutions
REASONING — creating strong arguments

"《世界思想宝库钥匙丛书》提供了独一无二的跨学科学习和研究工具。它介绍那些革新了各自学科研究的经典著作,还邀请全世界一流专家和教育机构进行严谨的分析,为每位读者打开世界顶级教育的大门。"

—— 安德烈亚斯·施莱歇尔,
经济合作与发展组织教育与技能司司长

"《世界思想宝库钥匙丛书》直面大学教育的巨大挑战……他们组建了一支精干而活跃的学者队伍,来推出在研究广度上颇具新意的教学材料。"

—— 布罗尔斯教授、勋爵,剑桥大学前校长

"《世界思想宝库钥匙丛书》的愿景令人赞叹。它通过分析和阐释那些曾深刻影响人类思想以及社会、经济发展的经典文本,提供了新的学习方法。它推动批判性思维,这对于任何社会和经济体来说都是至关重要的。这就是未来的学习方法。"

—— 查尔斯·克拉克阁下,英国前教育大臣

"对于那些影响了各自领域的著作,《世界思想宝库钥匙丛书》能让人们立即了解到围绕那些著作展开的评论性言论,这让该系列图书成为在这些领域从事研究的师生们不可或缺的资源。"

—— 威廉·特朗佐教授,加利福尼亚大学圣地亚哥分校

"Macat offers an amazing first-of-its-kind tool for interdisciplinary learning and research. Its focus on works that transformed their disciplines and its rigorous approach, drawing on the world's leading experts and educational institutions, opens up a world-class education to anyone."

—— Andreas Schleicher, Director for Education and Skills, Organisation for Economic Co-operation and Development

"Macat is taking on some of the major challenges in university education... They have drawn together a strong team of active academics who are producing teaching materials that are novel in the breadth of their approach."

—— Prof Lord Broers, former Vice-Chancellor of the University of Cambridge

"The Macat vision is exceptionally exciting. It focuses upon new modes of learning which analyse and explain seminal texts which have profoundly influenced world thinking and so social and economic development. It promotes the kind of critical thinking which is essential for any society and economy. This is the learning of the future."

—— Rt Hon Charles Clarke, former UK Secretary of State for Education

"The Macat analyses provide immediate access to the critical conversation surrounding the books that have shaped their respective discipline, which will make them an invaluable resource to all of those, students and teachers, working in the field."

—— Prof William Tronzo, University of California at San Diego

The Macat Library
世界思想宝库钥匙丛书

TITLE	中文书名	类别
An Analysis of Arjun Appadurai's *Modernity at Large: Cultural Dimensions of Globalisation*	解析阿尔君·阿帕杜莱《消失的现代性：全球化的文化维度》	人类学
An Analysis of Claude Lévi-Strauss's *Structural Anthropology*	解析克劳德·列维-斯特劳斯《结构人类学》	人类学
An Analysis of Marcel Mauss's *The Gift*	解析马塞尔·莫斯《礼物》	人类学
An Analysis of Jared M. Diamond's *Guns, Germs, and Steel: The Fate of Human Societies*	解析贾雷德·戴蒙德《枪炮、病菌与钢铁：人类社会的命运》	人类学
An Analysis of Clifford Geertz's *The Interpretation of Cultures*	解析克利福德·格尔茨《文化的解释》	人类学
An Analysis of Philippe Ariès's *Centuries of Childhood: A Social History of Family Life*	解析菲力浦·阿利埃斯《儿童的世纪：旧制度下的儿童和家庭生活》	人类学
An Analysis of W. Chan Kim & Renée Mauborgne's *Blue Ocean Strategy*	解析金伟灿/勒妮·莫博涅《蓝海战略》	商业
An Analysis of John P. Kotter's *Leading Change*	解析约翰·P.科特《领导变革》	商业
An Analysis of Michael E. Porter's *Competitive Strategy: Techniques for Analyzing Industries and Competitors*	解析迈克尔·E.波特《竞争战略：分析产业和竞争对手的技术》	商业
An Analysis of Jean Lave & Etienne Wenger's *Situated Learning: Legitimate Peripheral Participation*	解析琼·莱夫/艾蒂纳·温格《情境学习：合法的边缘性参与》	商业
An Analysis of Douglas McGregor's *The Human Side of Enterprise*	解析道格拉斯·麦格雷戈《企业的人性面》	商业
An Analysis of Milton Friedman's *Capitalism and Freedom*	解析米尔顿·弗里德曼《资本主义与自由》	商业
An Analysis of Ludwig von Mises's *The Theory of Money and Credit*	解析路德维希·冯·米塞斯《货币和信用理论》	经济学
An Analysis of Adam Smith's *The Wealth of Nations*	解析亚当·斯密《国富论》	经济学
An Analysis of Thomas Piketty's *Capital in the Twenty-First Century*	解析托马斯·皮凯蒂《21世纪资本论》	经济学
An Analysis of Nassim Nicholas Taleb's *The Black Swan: The Impact of the Highly Improbable*	解析纳西姆·尼古拉斯·塔勒布《黑天鹅：如何应对不可预知的未来》	经济学
An Analysis of Ha-Joon Chang's *Kicking Away the Ladder*	解析张夏准《富国陷阱：发达国家为何踢开梯子》	经济学
An Analysis of Thomas Robert Malthus's *An Essay on the Principle of Population*	解析托马斯·马尔萨斯《人口论》	经济学

An Analysis of John Maynard Keynes's *The General Theory of Employment, Interest and Money*	解析约翰·梅纳德·凯恩斯《就业、利息和货币通论》	经济学
An Analysis of Milton Friedman's *The Role of Monetary Policy*	解析米尔顿·弗里德曼《货币政策的作用》	经济学
An Analysis of Burton G. Malkiel's *A Random Walk Down Wall Street*	解析伯顿·G.马尔基尔《漫步华尔街》	经济学
An Analysis of Friedrich A. Hayek's *The Road to Serfdom*	解析弗里德里希·A.哈耶克《通往奴役之路》	经济学
An Analysis of Charles P. Kindleberger's *Manias, Panics, and Crashes: A History of Financial Crises*	解析查尔斯·P.金德尔伯格《疯狂、惊恐和崩溃：金融危机史》	经济学
An Analysis of Amartya Sen's *Development as Freedom*	解析阿马蒂亚·森《以自由看待发展》	经济学
An Analysis of Rachel Carson's *Silent Spring*	解析蕾切尔·卡森《寂静的春天》	地理学
An Analysis of Charles Darwin's *On the Origin of Species: by Means of Natural Selection, or The Preservation of Favoured Races in the Struggle for Life*	解析查尔斯·达尔文《物种起源》	地理学
An Analysis of World Commission on Environment and Development's *The Brundtland Report, Our Common Future*	解析世界环境与发展委员会《布伦特兰报告：我们共同的未来》	地理学
An Analysis of James E. Lovelock's *Gaia: A New Look at Life on Earth*	解析詹姆斯·E.拉伍拉克《盖娅：地球生命的新视野》	地理学
An Analysis of Paul Kennedy's *The Rise and Fall of the Great Powers: Economic Change and Military Conflict from 1500—2000*	解析保罗·肯尼迪《大国的兴衰：1500—2000年的经济变革与军事冲突》	历史
An Analysis of Janet L. Abu-Lughod's *Before European Hegemony: The World System A. D. 1250—1350*	解析珍妮特·L.阿布-卢格霍德《欧洲霸权之前：1250—1350年的世界体系》	历史
An Analysis of Alfred W. Crosby's *The Columbian Exchange: Biological and Cultural Consequences of 1492*	解析艾尔弗雷德·W.克罗斯比《哥伦布大交换：1492年以后的生物影响和文化冲击》	历史
An Analysis of Tony Judt's *Postwar: A History of Europe since 1945*	解析托尼·朱特《战后欧洲史》	历史
An Analysis of Richard J. Evans's *In Defence of History*	解析理查德·J.艾文斯《捍卫历史》	历史
An Analysis of Eric Hobsbawm's *The Age of Revolution: Europe 1789–1848*	解析艾瑞克·霍布斯鲍姆《革命的年代：欧洲1789—1848年》	历史

An Analysis of Roland Barthes's *Mythologies*	解析罗兰·巴特《神话学》	文学与批判理论
An Analysis of Simon de Beauvoir's *The Second Sex*	解析西蒙娜·德·波伏娃《第二性》	文学与批判理论
An Analysis of Edward W. Said's *Orientalism*	解析爱德华·W. 萨义德《东方主义》	文学与批判理论
An Analysis of Virginia Woolf's *A Room of One's Own*	解析弗吉尼亚·伍尔芙《一间自己的房间》	文学与批判理论
An Analysis of Judith Butler's *Gender Trouble*	解析朱迪斯·巴特勒《性别麻烦》	文学与批判理论
An Analysis of Ferdinand de Saussure's *Course in General Linguistics*	解析费尔迪南·德·索绪尔《普通语言学教程》	文学与批判理论
An Analysis of Susan Sontag's *On Photography*	解析苏珊·桑塔格《论摄影》	文学与批判理论
An Analysis of Walter Benjamin's *The Work of Art in the Age of Mechanical Reproduction*	解析瓦尔特·本雅明《机械复制时代的艺术作品》	文学与批判理论
An Analysis of W.E.B. Du Bois's *The Souls of Black Folk*	解析W.E.B. 杜波依斯《黑人的灵魂》	文学与批判理论
An Analysis of Plato's *The Republic*	解析柏拉图《理想国》	哲学
An Analysis of Plato's *Symposium*	解析柏拉图《会饮篇》	哲学
An Analysis of Aristotle's *Metaphysics*	解析亚里士多德《形而上学》	哲学
An Analysis of Aristotle's *Nicomachean Ethics*	解析亚里士多德《尼各马可伦理学》	哲学
An Analysis of Immanuel Kant's *Critique of Pure Reason*	解析伊曼努尔·康德《纯粹理性批判》	哲学
An Analysis of Ludwig Wittgenstein's *Philosophical Investigations*	解析路德维希·维特根斯坦《哲学研究》	哲学
An Analysis of G.W.F. Hegel's *Phenomenology of Spirit*	解析G.W.F. 黑格尔《精神现象学》	哲学
An Analysis of Baruch Spinoza's *Ethics*	解析巴鲁赫·斯宾诺莎《伦理学》	哲学
An Analysis of Hannah Arendt's *The Human Condition*	解析汉娜·阿伦特《人的境况》	哲学
An Analysis of G.E.M. Anscombe's *Modern Moral Philosophy*	解析G.E.M. 安斯康姆《现代道德哲学》	哲学
An Analysis of David Hume's *An Enquiry Concerning Human Understanding*	解析大卫·休谟《人类理解研究》	哲学

An Analysis of Søren Kierkegaard's *Fear and Trembling*	解析索伦·克尔凯郭尔《恐惧与战栗》	哲学
An Analysis of René Descartes's *Meditations on First Philosophy*	解析勒内·笛卡尔《第一哲学沉思录》	哲学
An Analysis of Friedrich Nietzsche's *On the Genealogy of Morality*	解析弗里德里希·尼采《论道德的谱系》	哲学
An Analysis of Gilbert Ryle's *The Concept of Mind*	解析吉尔伯特·赖尔《心的概念》	哲学
An Analysis of Thomas Kuhn's *The Structure of Scientific Revolutions*	解析托马斯·库恩《科学革命的结构》	哲学
An Analysis of John Stuart Mill's *Utilitarianism*	解析约翰·斯图亚特·穆勒《功利主义》	哲学
An Analysis of Aristotle's *Politics*	解析亚里士多德《政治学》	政治学
An Analysis of Niccolò Machiavelli's *The Prince*	解析尼科洛·马基雅维利《君主论》	政治学
An Analysis of Karl Marx's *Capital*	解析卡尔·马克思《资本论》	政治学
An Analysis of Benedict Anderson's *Imagined Communities*	解析本尼迪克特·安德森《想象的共同体》	政治学
An Analysis of Samuel P. Huntington's *The Clash of Civilizations and the Remaking of World Order*	解析塞缪尔·P.亨廷顿《文明的冲突与世界秩序重建》	政治学
An Analysis of Alexis de Tocqueville's *Democracy in America*	解析阿列克西·德·托克维尔《论美国的民主》	政治学
An Analysis of John A. Hobson's *Imperialism: A Study*	解析约翰·A.霍布森《帝国主义》	政治学
An Analysis of Thomas Paine's *Common Sense*	解析托马斯·潘恩《常识》	政治学
An Analysis of John Rawls's *A Theory of Justice*	解析约翰·罗尔斯《正义论》	政治学
An Analysis of Francis Fukuyama's *The End of History and the Last Man*	解析弗朗西斯·福山《历史的终结与最后的人》	政治学
An Analysis of John Locke's *Two Treatises of Government*	解析约翰·洛克《政府论》	政治学
An Analysis of Sun Tzu's *The Art of War*	解析孙武《孙子兵法》	政治学
An Analysis of Henry Kissinger's *World Order: Reflections on the Character of Nations and the Course of History*	解析亨利·基辛格《世界秩序》	政治学
An Analysis of Jean-Jacques Rousseau's *The Social Contract*	解析让-雅克·卢梭《社会契约论》	政治学

An Analysis of Odd Arne Westad's *The Global Cold War: Third World Interventions and the Making of Our Times*	解析文安立《全球冷战：美苏对第三世界的干涉与当代世界的形成》	政治学
An Analysis of Sigmund Freud's *The Interpretation of Dreams*	解析西格蒙德·弗洛伊德《梦的解析》	心理学
An Analysis of William James' *The Principles of Psychology*	解析威廉·詹姆斯《心理学原理》	心理学
An Analysis of Philip Zimbardo's *The Lucifer Effect*	解析菲利普·津巴多《路西法效应》	心理学
An Analysis of Leon Festinger's *A Theory of Cognitive Dissonance*	解析利昂·费斯汀格《认知失调论》	心理学
An Analysis of Richard H. Thaler & Cass R. Sunstein's *Nudge: Improving Decisions about Health, Wealth, and Happiness*	解析理查德·H. 泰勒/卡斯·R. 桑斯坦《助推：如何做出有关健康、财富和幸福的更优决策》	心理学
An Analysis of Gordon Allport's *The Nature of Prejudice*	解析高尔登·奥尔波特《偏见的本质》	心理学
An Analysis of Steven Pinker's *The Better Angels of Our Nature: Why Violence Has Declined*	解析斯蒂芬·平克《人性中的善良天使：暴力为什么会减少》	心理学
An Analysis of Stanley Milgram's *Obedience to Authority*	解析斯坦利·米尔格拉姆《对权威的服从》	心理学
An Analysis of Betty Friedan's *The Feminine Mystique*	解析贝蒂·弗里丹《女性的奥秘》	心理学
An Analysis of David Riesman's *The Lonely Crowd: A Study of the Changing American Character*	解析大卫·理斯曼《孤独的人群：美国人社会性格演变之研究》	社会学
An Analysis of Franz Boas's *Race, Language and Culture*	解析弗朗兹·博厄斯《种族、语言与文化》	社会学
An Analysis of Pierre Bourdieu's *Outline of a Theory of Practice*	解析皮埃尔·布尔迪厄《实践理论大纲》	社会学
An Analysis of Max Weber's *The Protestant Ethic and the Spirit of Capitalism*	解析马克斯·韦伯《新教伦理与资本主义精神》	社会学
An Analysis of Jane Jacobs's *The Death and Life of Great American Cities*	解析简·雅各布斯《美国大城市的死与生》	社会学
An Analysis of C. Wright Mills's *The Sociological Imagination*	解析 C. 赖特·米尔斯《社会学的想象力》	社会学
An Analysis of Robert E. Lucas Jr.'s *Why Doesn't Capital Flow from Rich to Poor Countries?*	解析小罗伯特·E. 卢卡斯《为何资本不从富国流向穷国？》	社会学

An Analysis of Émile Durkheim's *On Suicide*	解析埃米尔·迪尔凯姆《自杀论》	社会学
An Analysis of Eric Hoffer's *The True Believer: Thoughts on the Nature of Mass Movements*	解析埃里克·霍弗《狂热分子：群众运动圣经》	社会学
An Analysis of Jared M. Diamond's *Collapse: How Societies Choose to Fail or Survive*	解析贾雷德·M.戴蒙德《大崩溃：社会如何选择兴亡》	社会学
An Analysis of Michel Foucault's *The History of Sexuality Vol. 1: The Will to Knowledge*	解析米歇尔·福柯《性史（第一卷）：求知意志》	社会学
An Analysis of Michel Foucault's *Discipline and Punish*	解析米歇尔·福柯《规训与惩罚》	社会学
An Analysis of Richard Dawkins's *The Selfish Gene*	解析理查德·道金斯《自私的基因》	社会学
An Analysis of Antonio Gramsci's *Prison Notebooks*	解析安东尼奥·葛兰西《狱中札记》	社会学
An Analysis of Augustine's *Confessions*	解析奥古斯丁《忏悔录》	神学
An Analysis of C.S. Lewis's *The Abolition of Man*	解析C.S.路易斯《人之废》	神学

图书在版编目（CIP）数据

解析大卫·休谟《人类理解研究》/ 迈克·奥沙利文（Michael O'Sullivan）著. 王弋璇译 —上海：上海外语教育出版社，2019
（世界思想宝库钥匙丛书）
ISBN 978 - 7 - 5446 - 5871 - 3

Ⅰ. ①解… Ⅱ. ①迈… ②王… Ⅲ. ①休谟（Hume, David 1711—1776）—社会人类学—研究 Ⅳ. ①B561.291②C912.4

中国版本图书馆CIP数据核字（2019）第121713号

This Chinese-English bilingual edition of *An Analysis of David Hume's* An Enquiry Concerning Human Understanding is published by arrangement with Macat International Limited. Licensed for sale throughout the world.
本书汉英双语版由Macat国际有限公司授权上海外语教育出版社有限公司出版。供在全世界范围内发行、销售。

图字：09 - 2018 - 549

出版发行：**上海外语教育出版社**
（上海外国语大学内） 邮编：200083
电　　话：021-65425300（总机）
电子邮箱：bookinfo@sflep.com.cn
网　　址：http://www.sflep.com
责任编辑：唐小春

印　　刷：上海市崇明县裕安印刷厂
开　　本：890×1240　1/32　印张 5　字数 102千字
版　　次：2019 年 8 月第 1 版　2019 年 8 月第 1 次印刷
印　　数：2 100 册

书　　号：ISBN 978-7-5446-5871-3 / B
定　　价：30.00 元
本版图书如有印装质量问题，可向本社调换
质量服务热线：4008-213-263　电子邮箱：editorial@sflep.com